Map Skills Made Fun:
Neighborhoods and Communities

60 Fun and Engaging Reproducibles That Teach Key Map Skills
and Invite Kids to Learn About Urban, Suburban, and Rural Communities

by Catherine M. Tamblyn

S C H O L A S T I C
PROFESSIONAL BOOKS

NEW YORK • TORONTO • LONDON • AUCKLAND • SYDNEY • MEXICO CITY
NEW DELHI • HONG KONG • BUENOS AIRES

Dedication

To Peter and Andrew for your continued support.

Scholastic Inc. grants teachers permission to photocopy the activity sheets from this book for classroom use. No other part of this publication may be reproduced in whole or in part, or stored in a retrieval system, or transmitted in any form or by any means, electronic, mechanical, photocopying, recording, or otherwise, without written permission of the publisher. For information regarding permission, write to Scholastic Inc., 557 Broadway, New York, NY 10012.

Cover design by Josué Castilleja
Cover illustration by Bonnie Mathews
Interior design by Russell Cohen
Interior illustrations by James Graham Hale

ISBN 0-439-29643-9

1 2 3 4 5 6 7 8 9 10   40   08 07 06 05 04 03 02

TABLE OF CONTENTS

PART ONE: In the City

PART TWO: Surrounding Suburbs

PART THREE: In the Country

Introduction

Welcome to *Map Skills Made Fun: Neighborhoods and Communities!*
The engaging, reproducible activities in this book offer a great supplement to your social studies curriculum. Students will enjoy exploring urban, suburban, and rural communities as they develop geography and mapping skills.

This book is divided into three parts: **In the City** (featuring urban communities), **Surrounding Suburbs** (communities on the outskirts of cities), and **In the Country** (rural communities and the countryside). Each section portrays views and elements of the particular community that you won't see in conventional social studies textbooks. For each community, you'll find fun and ready-to-go skills pages that feature different kinds of maps, such as neighborhood, coordinate, floor plan, and political maps. Students will learn how to read and use map symbols, keys, indexes, and compass roses. They'll also learn key map concepts such as location, perspective, scale, map making, and following directions.

How to Use This Book
Most of the activities in this book are single-page reproducibles that stand on their own. A few activities, however, require two or more activity pages that can be assembled together into Map Mini-Packs, as identified below. You may want to staple or clip the pages for each mini-pack together before distributing them to students.

City Map Mini-Packs
- Eight Steps to City Park (pages 15–17)
- Blocks and Lots (pages 19–20, 74–75)
- A Step Away (pages 23, 69)
- Fun Run (pages 24, 69)
- City Block (pages 25–26, 72–76)
- City Planner (pages 27–29, 72–76)

Suburb Map Mini-Packs
- Wild Water Park (pages 37, 71)
- Wheels Away (pages 42, 69)
- Road Rally (pages 43, 69)
- Superb Suburb (pages 45–47, 72–76)

Country Map Mini-Packs
- From Eagles' Eyes (pages 48–49)
- Dino Dig (pages 54, 17)
- Directions in Directions (pages 58–59)
- Busting Big Air (pages 60, 70)
- Desert Sculptures (pages 62, 70)
- Camp Winaped (pages 63, 70)
- Rockland's Ranches (pages 64, 70)
- Country Community (pages 65–67, 72–76)
- Three Communities Fit-Together Map (pages 28–29, 46–47, 66–67, 68, 72–76)

 You can also group the activity pages in this book according to the map skills they reinforce (see below). As with the Map Mini-Packs, you can assemble the reproducible pages for each map skill and offer them to students as Map Skills Packs. This is a great way to provide skills practice, assess individual strengths and weaknesses, or offer extra credit.

Coordinate Map Skills Pack
- Zany Zoo (page 14)
- Eight Steps to City Park (pages 15–17)
- Twin Lakes (page 36)
- Wild Water Park (page 37)
- Down on the Farm (page 53)
- Dino Dig (page 54)
- Cool Coordinates (page 17)

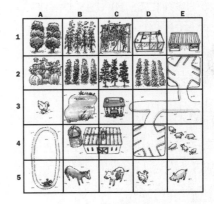

Direction Map Skills Pack
- Catch That Bus! (page 18)
- Blocks and Lots (pages 19–20)
- City to City (page 22)
- Fun Run (page 24)
- Firefighters' Fair (page 38)
- Town Center (page 39)
- Town to Town (page 41)

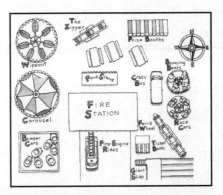

- White Water (page 55)
- Tracking Trails (page 56)
- Directions in Directions (pages 58–59)
- Three Peaks (page 61)
- Compass Roses (page 73)

Location Map Skills Pack
- Pigeon's Perch (page 9)
- Which Hotel? (page 12)
- Missing Exhibits (page 13)
- Pirate's Cove Playground (page 33)
- Kids' Camp Out (page 34)
- Smart Shopper (page 35)
- On Main Street (page 51)
- Saddle Up (page 52)

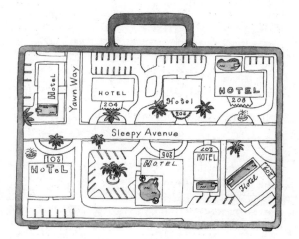

Pre-Scale/Scale Map Skills Pack
- City Sightseer (page 21)
- City to City (page 22)
- A Step Away (page 23)
- Fun Run (page 24)
- Perfect Pathways (page 40)
- Town to Town (page 41)
- Wheels Away (page 42)
- Road Rally (page 43)
- Busting Big Air (page 60)
- Three Peaks (page 61)
- Desert Sculptures (page 62)
- Camp Winaped (page 63)
- Rockland's Ranches (page 64)
- Cut-Out Rulers (pages 69–70)

 Another way to group the activities is through the different types of maps. For example, you can put together all the floor plans (pages 13, 35, and 52) or political maps (pages 22, 41, and 61) from the different sections of the book.

A tri-communities tour awaits you and your class. Enjoy the sights!

Name _____   **Date** _____

Pigeon's Perch

There are many ways to look at things.

| A city tree might look like this from afar. | The same tree would look this way from under it. | A pigeon flying above the tree would see it this way. |

Places and things on the city map below look the way a pigeon would see them from above. Can you tell what the places and things are from this view? Draw lines to match the words to pictures on the map.

parking lot   park   apartment   store

City Neighborhood

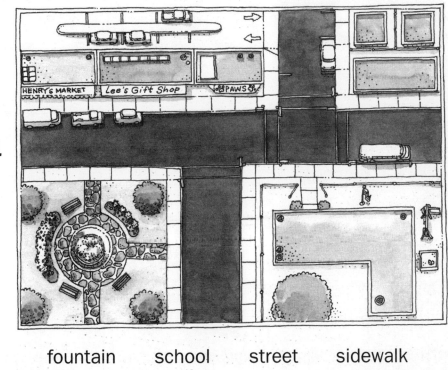

fountain   school   street   sidewalk

City Sign Language

Many city signs use a language all people can understand.
This language uses picture symbols. The symbols tell about real places and where
they are found. Match each picture symbol with the place that it stands for.

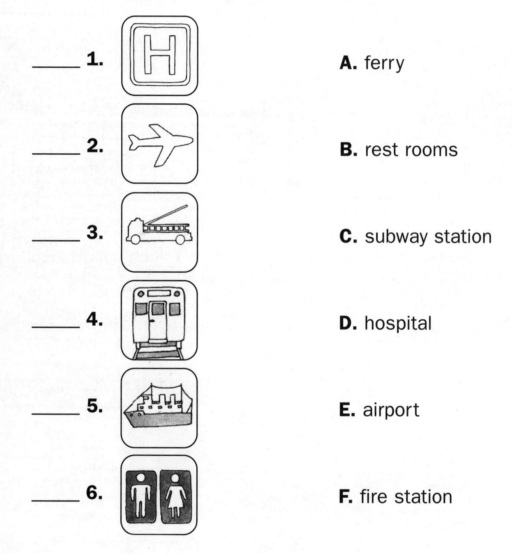

_____ 1.　　　　　　　　**A.** ferry

_____ 2.　　　　　　　　**B.** rest rooms

_____ 3.　　　　　　　　**C.** subway station

_____ 4.　　　　　　　　**D.** hospital

_____ 5.　　　　　　　　**E.** airport

_____ 6.　　　　　　　　**F.** fire station

Make up your own symbols for these places.

park　　　　**post office**　　　　**library**　　　　**office building**

Picture This

Greetings from Skyscraper City! The picture symbols around this postcard quickly tell you about some places in this city. Use the map key below to learn what the shape symbols stand for. Then draw a map of Skyscraper City below.

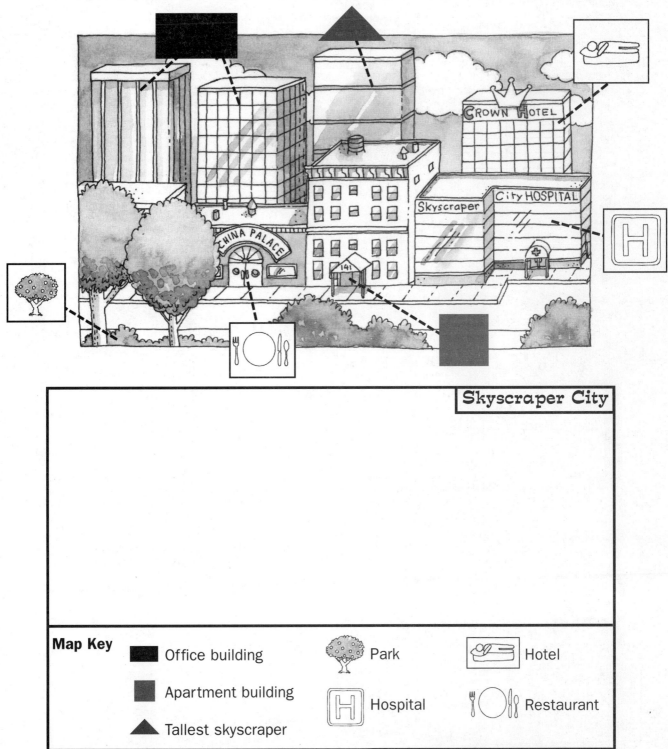

Skyscraper City

Map Key

- ▪ Office building
- ▪ Apartment building
- ▲ Tallest skyscraper
- 🌳 Park
- H Hospital
- 🍽 Hotel
- 🍴 Restaurant

Which Hotel?

It's getting late and the Smith family needs to find their hotel.
They know it's in Slumber City, but which hotel is it? Use the facts below
to find their hotel before everyone falls asleep!

Facts

✔ The hotel has a parking lot behind it.
✔ The hotel is not on Yawn Way.
✔ The hotel has an outside pool.
✔ The hotel is between two others with circular driveways.
✔ The hotel is between two palm trees.

1. Which hotel is the Smith's?

_____

2. What is the hotel's street address?

_____

Missing Exhibits

The American Museum is missing six exhibits. Cut out the exhibits at the right of the page. Then follow the directions to paste them on the floor plan.

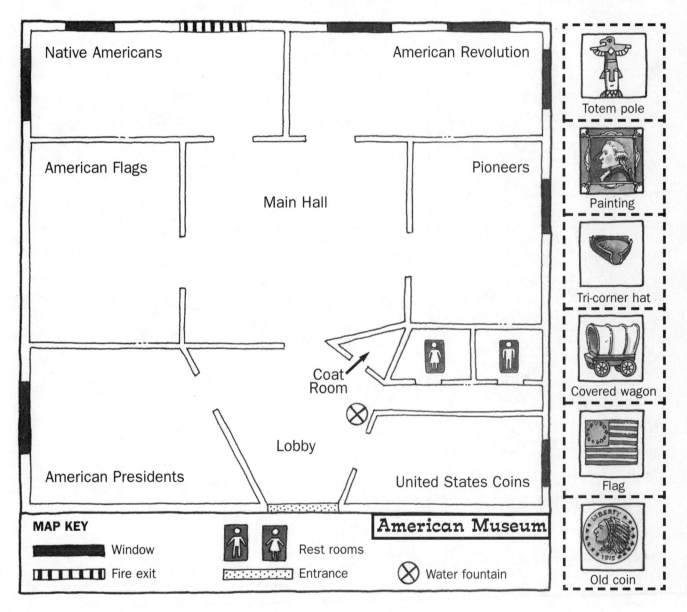

1. Put the totem pole in the room with a fire exit.
2. Put the painting in the room to the left of the lobby.
3. Put the hat in the room with three windows.
4. Put the covered wagon in the room to the right of the Main Hall.
5. Put the flag in the room with no windows.
6. Put the coin in the room to the right of the water fountain.

Zany Zoo

Grid maps have letters and numbers called *coordinates*. The coordinates name each square on the map. They help locate places and things on the map.
Find Zany Zoo's entrance. It's at 5–A.

Map Index

Birds	2–B
Brown bears	5–B
Chimps	4–A
Elephants	2–D
Entrance	5–A
Food stand	3–B
Gift shop	2–C
Giraffes	1–D
Gorillas	3–A
Hippos	1–C
Lions	1–B
Penguins	5–C
Picnic area	4–B
Polar bears	4–D
Reptiles	3–D
Rest rooms	3–C
Rhinos	2–A
Seals	5–D
Water fountain	4–C
Zebras	1–A

The map of Zany Zoo is missing some animals. Use the map index above to see which animals are missing. Then draw them in the correct places on the map.

Eight Steps to City Park*

You can make a city park grid map in eight easy steps.
Check the box after you've finished each step.

❏ **Step 1:** Cut out the "Cool Coordinates" grid map on page 17.

❏ **Step 2:** Cut out the map key and index on page 16.

❏ **Step 3:** Paste the grid map, map key, and map index on large construction paper.

❏ **Step 4:** Cut apart the City Park Symbols on page 16.

❏ **Step 5:** Paste the symbols on your map. Use the map index to find out where things go.

❏ **Step 6:** Draw symbols for these things on your map:
- 4 benches
- 2 water fountains
- 3 statues

❏ **Step 7:** Write the coordinates in the map index for each symbol you drew.

❏ **Step 8:** Write the name of your city park in the title box below the grid.

*Use with pages 16–17.

Name _____ **Date** _____

City Park Map Key and Index*

Use the map key and index to make a city park grid map.
Follow the directions on "Eight Steps to City Park."

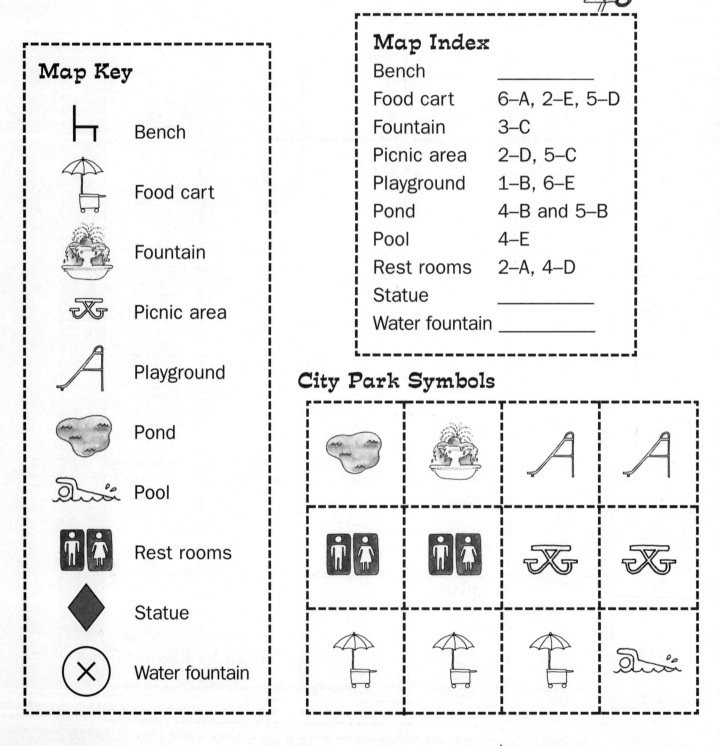

Map Key

⊢ Bench

☂ Food cart

⛲ Fountain

Picnic area

Playground

Pond

Pool

Rest rooms

◆ Statue

ⓧ Water fountain

Map Index

Bench	_____
Food cart	6–A, 2–E, 5–D
Fountain	3–C
Picnic area	2–D, 5–C
Playground	1–B, 6–E
Pond	4–B and 5–B
Pool	4–E
Rest rooms	2–A, 4–D
Statue	_____
Water fountain	_____

City Park Symbols

Cool Coordinates*

Make your own grid map. Just add a map key, index, and symbols.

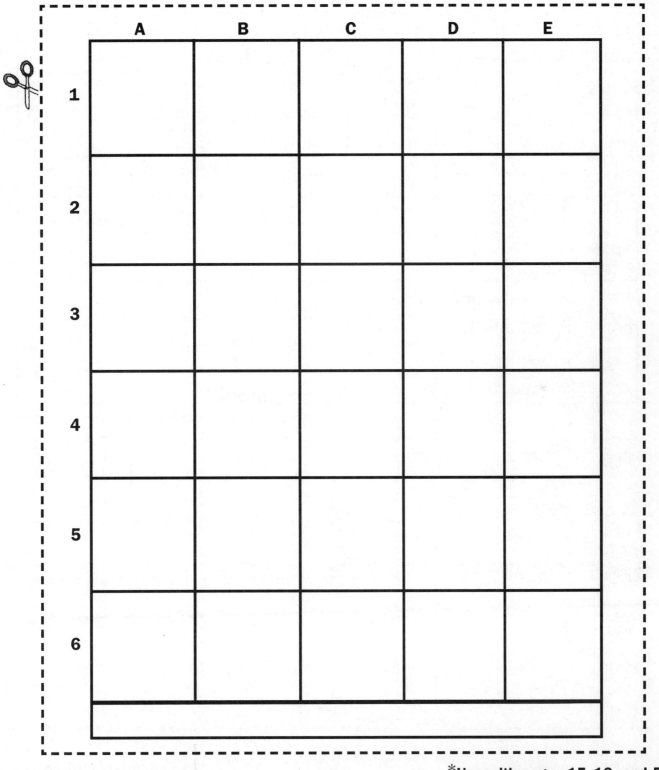

*Use with pages 15–16, and 54.

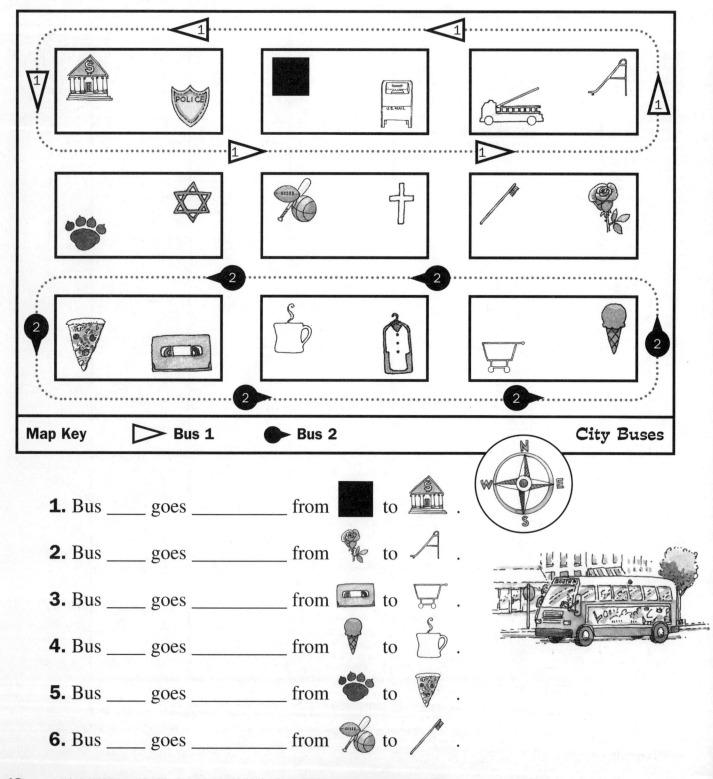

Catch That Bus!

Hitch a ride on a city bus. Find the different places on the map. Write the bus number that takes you from place to place. Then write the direction the bus is going.

Map Key ▷ **Bus 1** ● **Bus 2** **City Buses**

1. Bus _____ goes _____ from ■ to 🏛 .

2. Bus _____ goes _____ from 🌹 to A .

3. Bus _____ goes _____ from 📼 to 🛒 .

4. Bus _____ goes _____ from 🍦 to ☕ .

5. Bus _____ goes _____ from 🐾 to 🍕 .

6. Bus _____ goes _____ from ⚾ to 🪥 .

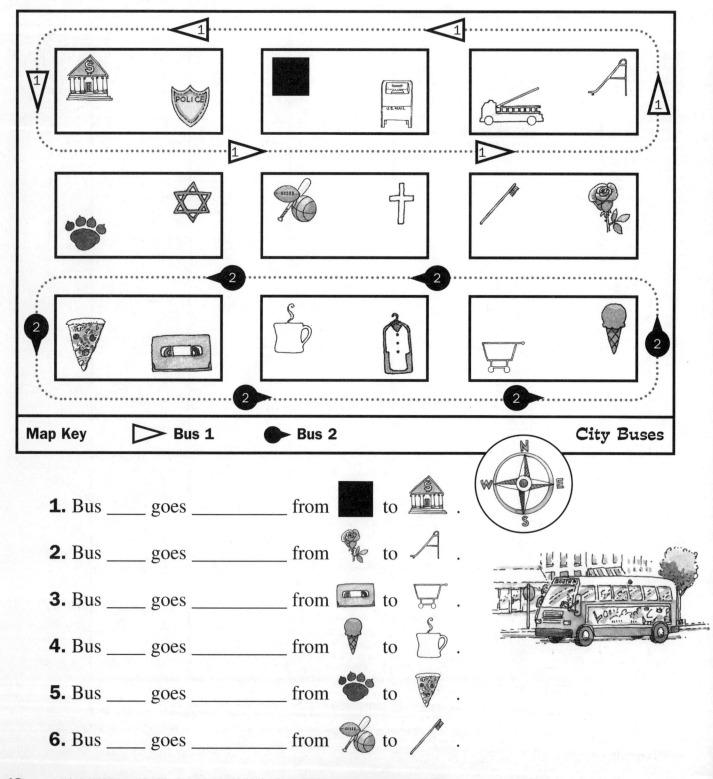

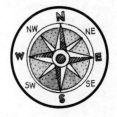

Blocks and Lots*

Create a city map using the "Blocks and Lots Map" on page 20 and
the map symbols on pages 74–75. Follow the directions below to make the map.
Mark each circle with an X after you add the symbol to your map.

○ A food store is N of the hotel.

○ A bank is in the NW corner of Lot 2.

○ A pizza parlor is in the SE corner of Lot 2.

○ A library is in Lot 3, NE of the pizza parlor.

○ A gas station is in Lot 2, W of the library.

○ A school is S of the library in Lot 3.

○ A music shop is in Lot 6, E of the park.

○ A toy store is S of the music shop in Lot 6.

○ A café is on Avenue C in the SW corner of Lot 5.

○ A bike shop is S of the café in the NW corner of Lot 7.

○ A police station is in the SE corner of Lot 7.

○ A post office is on Avenue D, W of the police station.

○ A pet shop is N of the sports store in Lot 4.

○ A fire station is in Lot 4, SW of the cafe.

*Use with pages 20 and 74–75.

Blocks and Lots Map*

Follow the directions on page 19 to create a city map below.

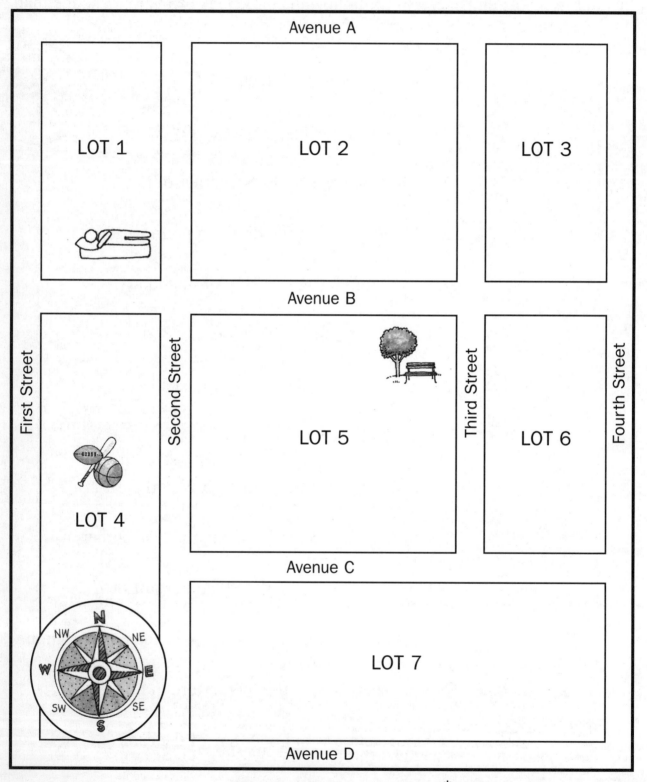

*Use with pages 19 and 74–75.

Name _____ **Date** _____

City Sightseer

Silver City sightseers can take a hansom cab ride to tour nine sites.
Count the horseshoe symbols to see how long a ride between these sites takes.

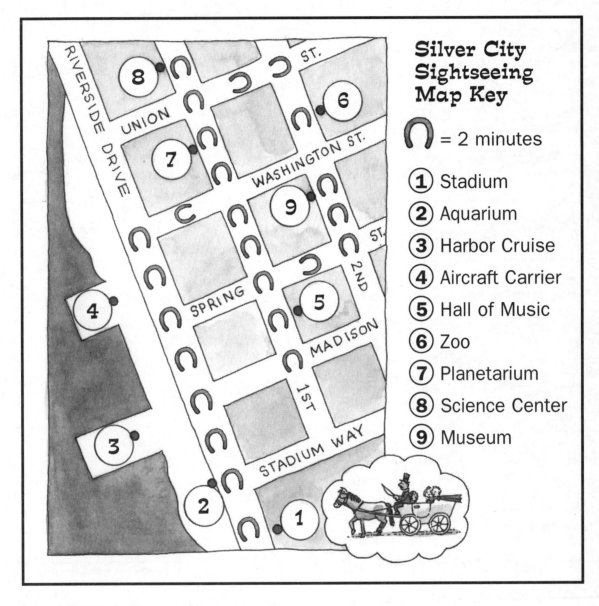

Silver City
Sightseeing
Map Key

∩ = 2 minutes

① Stadium
② Aquarium
③ Harbor Cruise
④ Aircraft Carrier
⑤ Hall of Music
⑥ Zoo
⑦ Planetarium
⑧ Science Center
⑨ Museum

1. Stadium to Harbor Cruise: _____ minutes

2. Science Center to Zoo: _____ minutes

3. Hall of Music to Museum: _____ minutes

4. Aircraft Carrier to Aquarium: _____ minutes

5. Planetarium to Aquarium going by 1st, Washington Street,
and Riverside Drive: _____ minutes

City to City

Rainbow County has 12 colorful cities. The number of miles from city to city is shown on the map.

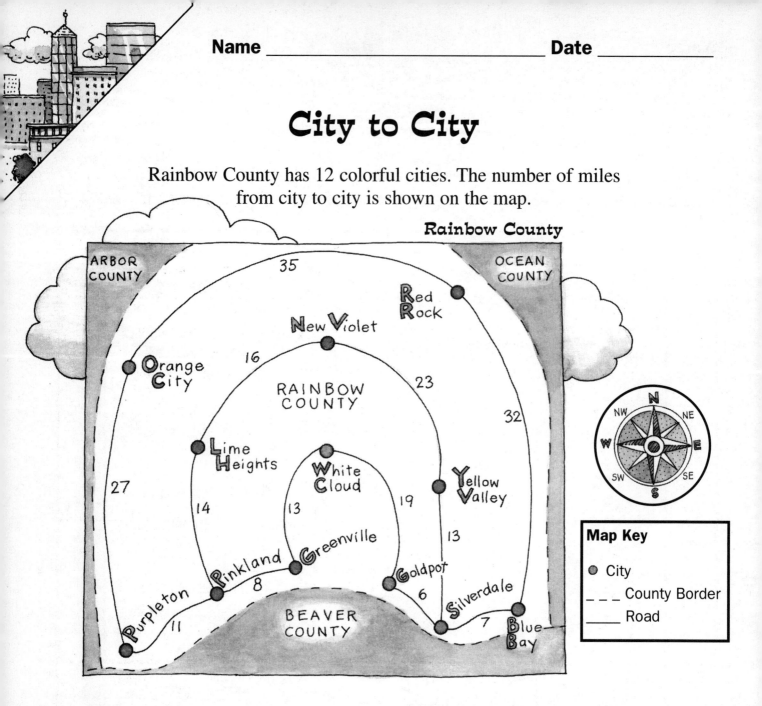

Write the number of miles between these cities:

1. New Violet to Lime Heights _____

2. Orange City to Red Rock _____

3. Blue Bay to Goldpot _____

4. Purpleton to Greenville _____

Write the direction from one city to the other:

5. White Cloud is _____ of New Violet.

6. Orange City is _____ of Purpleton.

7. Yellow Valley is _____ of Greenville.

8. Lime Heights is _____ of Silverdale.

Write the name of the city:

9. _____ is near the <u>northeast</u> county border.

10. _____ is near the <u>southwest</u> county border.

A Step Away

Have you ever counted your footsteps to measure the distance from one place to another? Use the Step Ruler on page 69 to count the footsteps between places on this map. Draw a line from the ✖ to the ●. Measure the line to find the number of inches. The map scale tells how many footsteps equal one inch.

City Steps

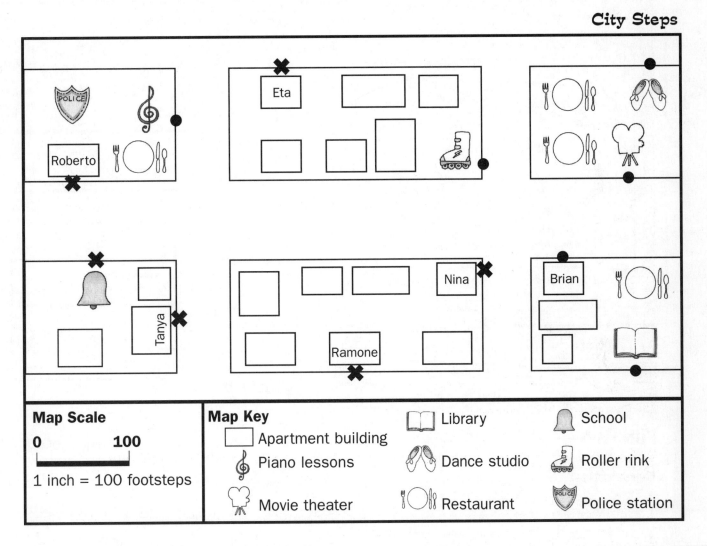

Map Scale

0   100

1 inch = 100 footsteps

Map Key

▢ Apartment building
🎼 Piano lessons
🎬 Movie theater

📖 Library
🩰 Dance studio
🍴◯🍴 Restaurant

🔔 School
Roller rink
Police station

1. _____ footsteps from Ramone's building to the library.

2. _____ footsteps from Brian's building to the school.

3. _____ footsteps from Tanya's building to piano lessons.

4. _____ footsteps from Roberto's building to the movie theater.

5. _____ footsteps from Eta's building to the dance studio.

6. _____ footsteps from Nina's building to the roller rink.

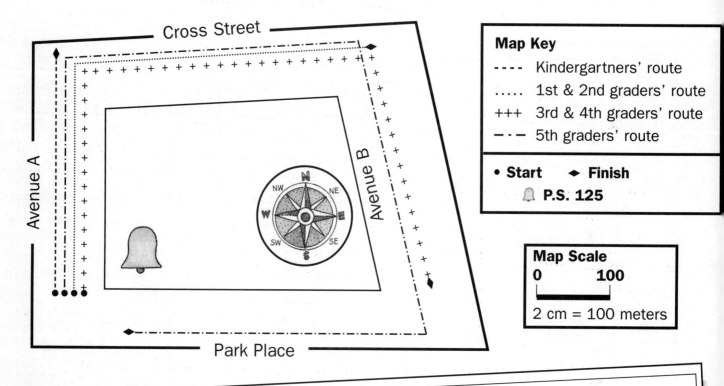

Fun Run

P.S. 125 just had their "Run for Fun" event! Read all about it in their school newsletter below. Then use the map and the Fun Run Ruler (page 69) to fill in the blanks of the newsletter.

Cross Street

Avenue A

Avenue B

Park Place

Map Key

- - - -   Kindergartners' route

.....   1st & 2nd graders' route

+++   3rd & 4th graders' route

— · —   5th graders' route

• **Start**   ◆ **Finish**

🔔 **P.S. 125**

Map Scale

0   100

2 cm = 100 meters

P.S. 125's Newsletter

Fun Run

P.S. 125's "Run for Fun" took place on October 2. All runners met at the corner of Avenue A and Park Place. Kindergartners started the fun, running _____ meters north on _____. Runners in 1st and 2nd grades ran on Avenue A. Then they turned northeast on _____ for a total of _____ meters. Runners in 3rd and 4th grades ran the same route. But they continued southeast on _____ for a total of _____ meters. The 5th grade run was _____ meters! The last leg of their route brought them west into a cheering crowd. Congratulations to all runners! on _____

City Block*

A city neighborhood is often made up of one street or block. The neighborhood might be made up of all houses or it could have a mix of houses, apartment buildings, and other city places.

Map your own city neighborhood using:

• City Block Map (page 26)
• Blank map key (page 72)
• Compass rose (page 73)
• Map symbols (pages 74–76)

Map Directions: Check each box as you complete the step.

❏ **1.** Paste a compass rose on the City Block Map.
❏ **2.** Paste the map key to your map.
❏ **3.** Draw a street on your map.
❏ **4.** Think of a name for the street and label it.
❏ **5.** Add a sidewalk on both sides of the street.
❏ **6.** Cut out symbols for places you want to show and paste them along the street. You might use ⌂ to stand for a home. Different colors of the same symbol can stand for homes of different families. For example:

Ricardo's house   Keisha's house   Ulanda's house

❏ **7.** Add your own symbols for trees, bushes, and gardens. Add symbols for parking lots, fences, and streetlights.
❏ **8.** Show all your symbols in the map key and label them.
❏ **9.** Write a title for your map in the title box.
❏ **10.** Write some questions about your map for a friend to answer.

*Use with pages 26 and 72–76.

City Block Map*

Make a map of a city neighborhood here.
Follow the directions on "City Block," page 25.

*Use with pages 25 and 72–75.

City Planner*

A new city needs to be built and you're the one planning it!
A good way to plan the city is to map it.

Make a Map

1. Paste or tape the Fit-Together City Map (pages 28–29) side by side.

2. Cut out the blank map key from page 72. Paste it to the bottom of your map.

3. Paste a compass rose from page 73 to the map.

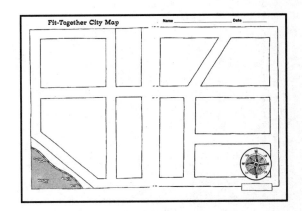

Add Symbols and Details

1. Look at the map symbols on pages 74–76. Cut out and paste the symbols you wish to use on your map. You might use abstract symbols for these city buildings:

 office buildings △ apartment buildings ☐ houses

Choose the best spot for each place. For example, you probably won't want an airport too close to a neighborhood.

2. Show all your map symbols in the key. Write what each symbol stands for.

3. Name your roads. Some roads use these words:

Route   Street   Avenue   Lane   Road   Way   Highway   Boulevard

4. Finally, name your city. Write its name in the title box.

*Use with pages 28–29 and 72–76.

Fit-Together City Map

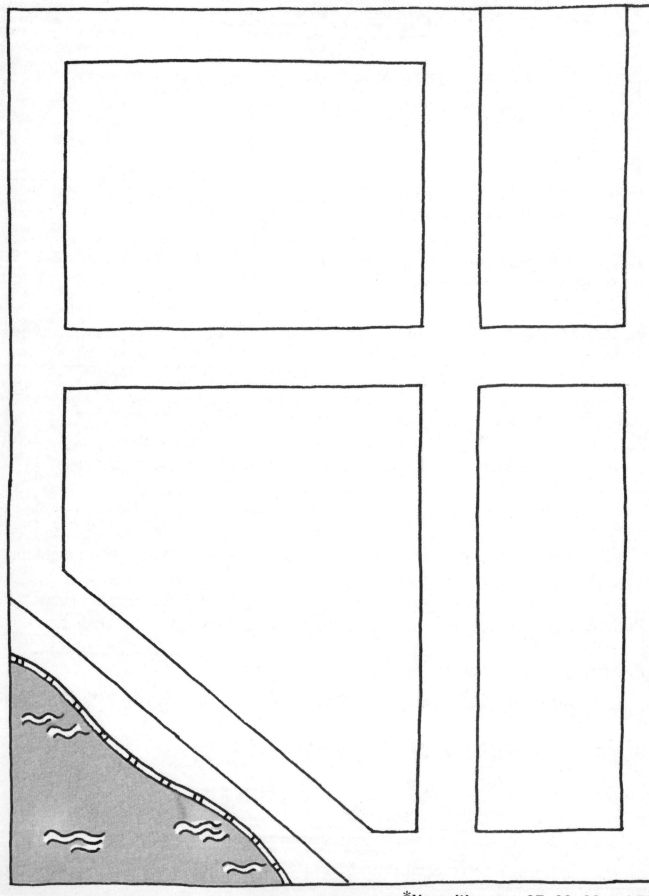

*Use with pages 27, 29, 68 and 72–76.

Name _____ **Date** _____

Title

Name _____ **Date** _____

Spying Sparrow

A sparrow is spying on two neighbors from above. It sees Jenna reading in her yard. It sees José watering flowers in his yard.

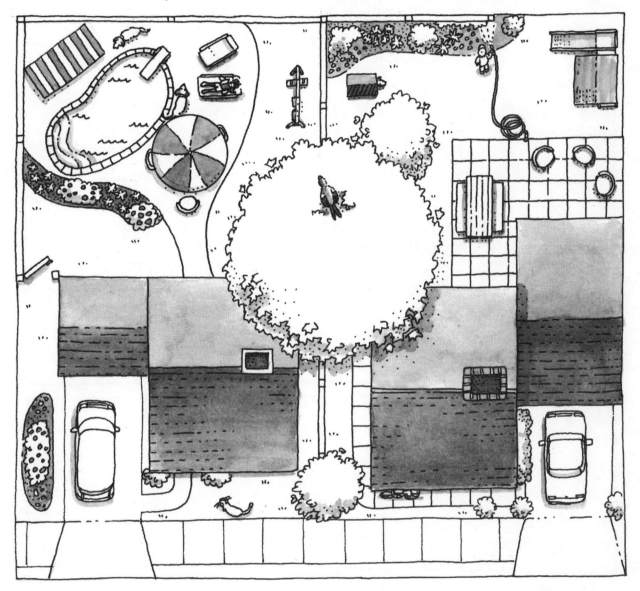

Play "I Spy" like the sparrow. Write how many of each thing you see from the sparrow's view.

_____ pool	_____ slide	_____ tree
_____ dog	_____ car	_____ picnic table
_____ cat	_____ umbrella	_____ swing set
_____ dog house	_____ flower garden	_____ chimney

Picture Perfect

Part of a picture-perfect neighborhood is shown on the postcard.
Make a map of this place using the symbols in the key. Think of a name
for your map. Write it in the title box.

Map Key

■ Home   ⌂ Bush   Restaurant

○ Tree   Ice-cream parlor   // Sidewalk

Name _____ **Date** _____

Pirate's Cove Playground

Use the map and key to tell where things are on Pirate's Cove Playground.

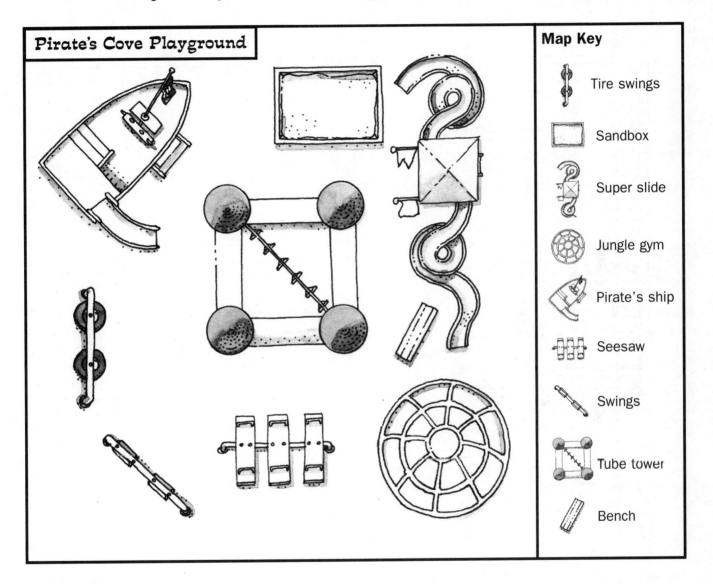

1. The _____ is in the <u>middle</u> of the playground.

2. The jungle gym is to the <u>right</u> of the _____.

3. The _____ is to the <u>left</u> of the sandbox.

4. The _____ are <u>between</u> the pirate ship and the swings.

5. Two flags are <u>on</u> the _____.

Kids' Camp Out

Corey and his friends are camping. Use the facts below and the map key
to draw symbols on the map. Add the same symbols to the key.
Be sure to make each boy's tent look different.

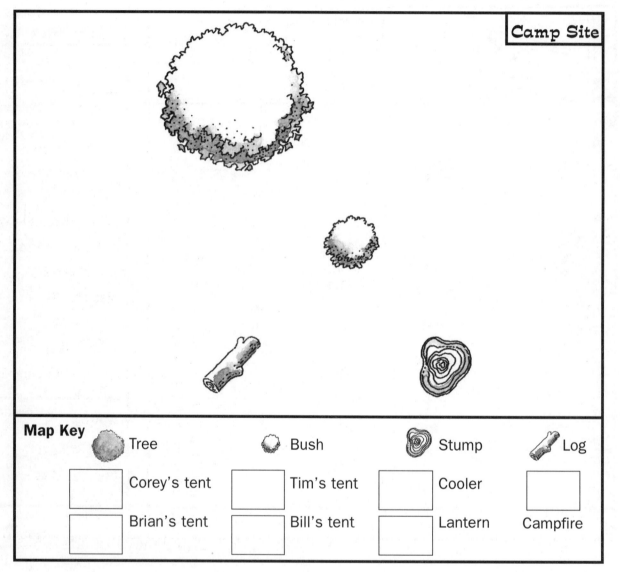

Camp Site

Map Key   Tree   Bush   Stump   Log

| | Corey's tent | | Tim's tent | | Cooler | | Log |
| | Brian's tent | | Bill's tent | | Lantern | Campfire |

- Corey's tent is to the <u>right</u> of the tree.
- Brian's tent is to the <u>left</u> of the same tree.
- Bill's tent is to the <u>right</u> of the bush.
- Tim's tent is <u>between</u> Bill's and Corey's tent.
- A campfire is to the <u>left</u> of the bush.
- A lantern is <u>on</u> the stump.
- A cooler is <u>between</u> the big log and the stump.

Smart Shopper

A mall is a large building with many stores. A floor-plan map, like the one below, helps shoppers find places in the building. Use this floor plan to find your way around the Minton Mini Mall.

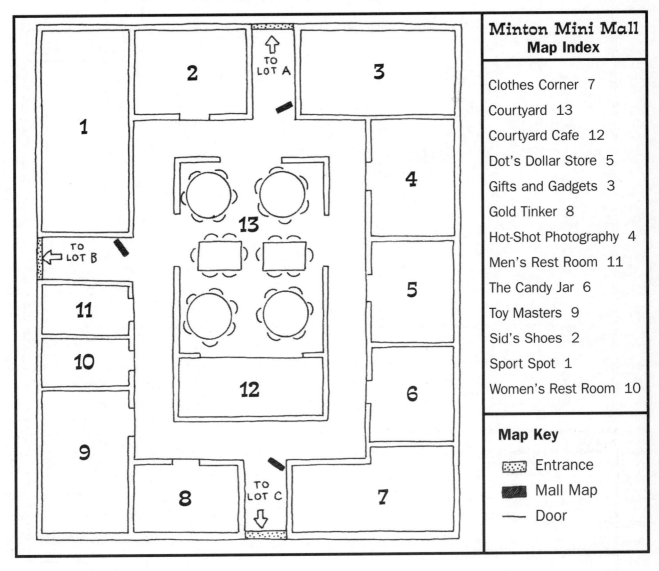

Minton Mini Mall
Map Index

Clothes Corner 7
Courtyard 13
Courtyard Cafe 12
Dot's Dollar Store 5
Gifts and Gadgets 3
Gold Tinker 8
Hot-Shot Photography 4
Men's Rest Room 11
The Candy Jar 6
Toy Masters 9
Sid's Shoes 2
Sport Spot 1
Women's Rest Room 10

Map Key

▨ Entrance
▧ Mall Map
— Door

1. What is store 6? _____

2. In what store could you buy a toy? _____

3. What store is next to Gifts and Gadgets? _____

4. Where could you shop for shoes? _____

5. Which store is next to the entrance for Parking Lot B? _____

6. How many mall maps are there? _____

Twin Lakes

Use the grid map to answer the questions below.

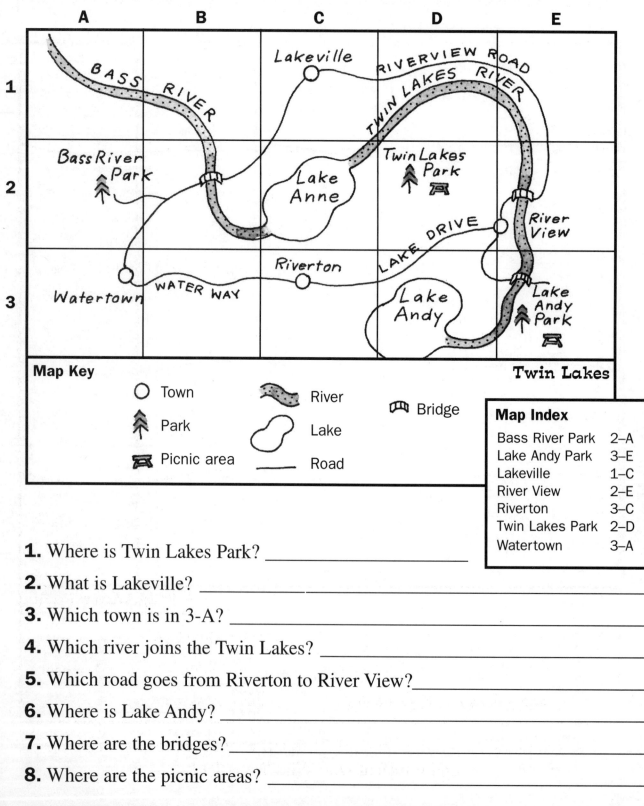

1. Where is Twin Lakes Park? _____

2. What is Lakeville? _____

3. Which town is in 3-A? _____

4. Which river joins the Twin Lakes? _____

5. Which road goes from Riverton to River View?_____

6. Where is Lake Andy? _____

7. Where are the bridges? _____

8. Where are the picnic areas? _____

Name _____ **Date** _____

Wild Water Park

Water parks are fun places to visit! Use the map and key to design your very own water park. Add some of your own ideas to the map and key.

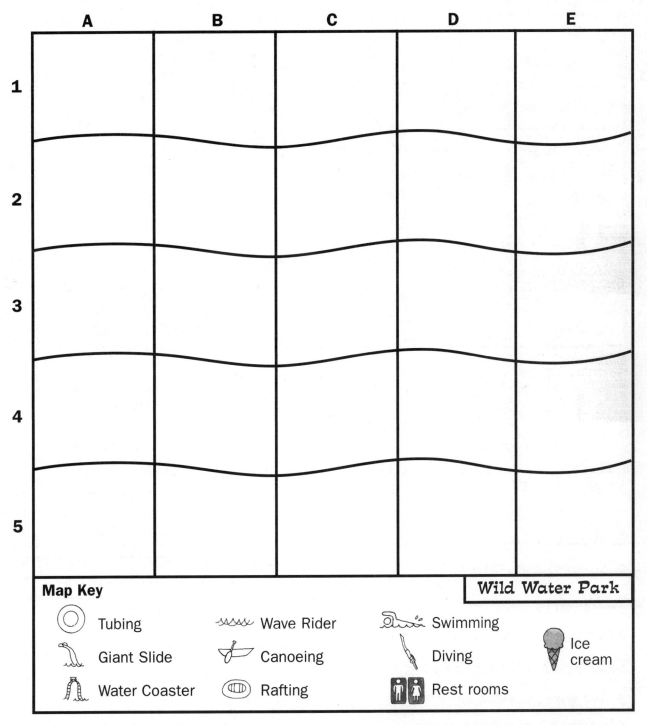

	A	B	C	D	E
1					
2					
3					
4					
5					

Map Key

Wild Water Park

◎ Tubing   〜〜 Wave Rider   ≈ Swimming

〜 Giant Slide   ⟡ Canoeing   ⎰ Diving   🍦 Ice cream

⚲ Water Coaster   ⬭ Rafting   🚻 Rest rooms

Use the blank map index on page 71 to tell about the location of places and things at your Wild Water Park.

Firefighters' Fair

Fair Haven's firefighters are holding a fair. Use the compass rose on the map to find the directions of places on the fairground.

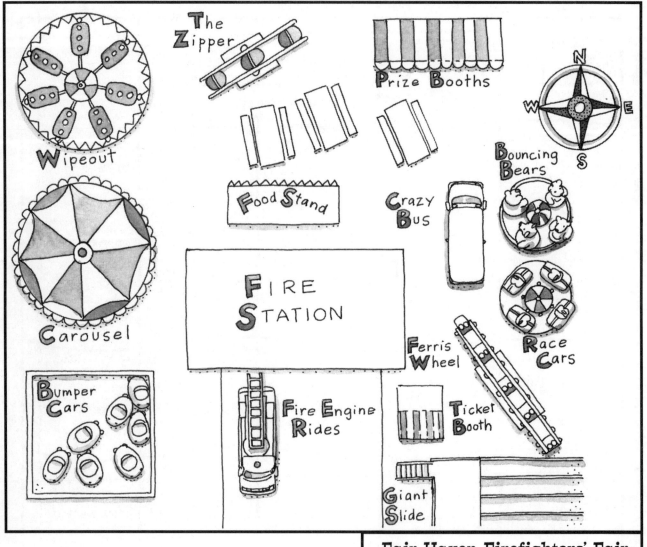

Fair Haven Firefighters' Fair

1. The food stand is _____ of the fire station.

2. The ticket booth is _____ of the Ferris wheel.

3. The prize booths are _____ of the Zipper.

4. The giant slide is _____ of the bumper cars.

5. Fire engine rides are _____ of the fire station.

6. The Crazy Bus is _____ of the Bouncing Bears ride.

Name _____ **Date** _____

Town Center

At the center of Terrytown is the town hall. You'll find it east of Center Street.
Use the compass rose to find the directions of other places in Terrytown.

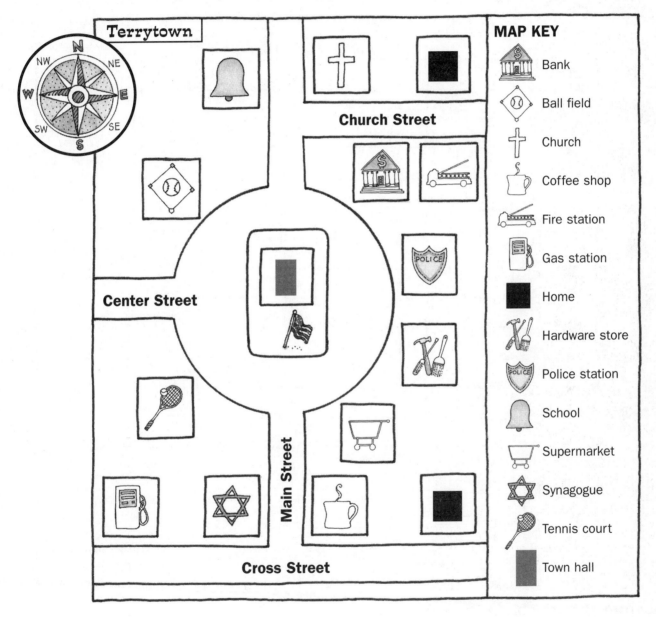

1. The bank is _____ of the town hall.
2. The school is _____ of the church.
3. The coffee shop is _____ of the synagogue.
4. Church Street is _____ of Cross Street.
5. A tennis court is _____ of the fire station.
6. The ball field is _____ of the hardware store.

Perfect Pathways

What is the shortest pathway to each place? Count the squares to find out.

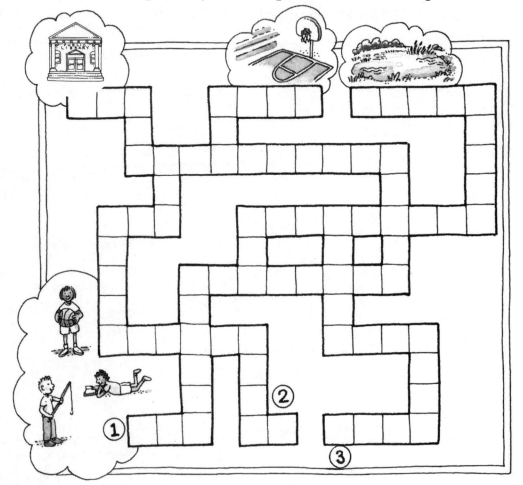

1. From ① to the library _____
2. From ② to the library _____
3. From ③ to the library _____
4. From ① to the basketball court _____
5. From ② to the basketball court _____
6. From ③ to the basketball court _____
7. From ① to the pond _____
8. From ② to the pond _____
9. From ③ to the pond _____
10. Which is the shortest path Jen can take to the library? _____
11. Which is the shortest path Julie can take to the court? _____
12. Which is the shortest path Jay can take to the pond? _____

Name _____ **Date** _____

Town to Town

Arbor County is famous for its tree-lined towns. The number of miles from town to town is shown on the map.

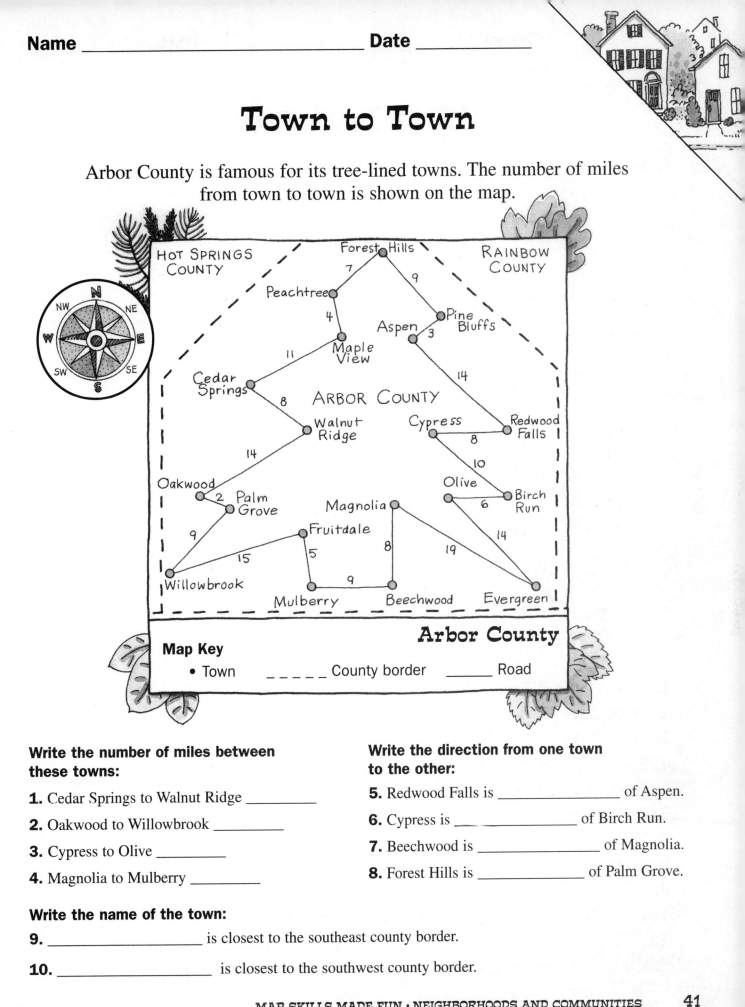

Write the number of miles between these towns:

1. Cedar Springs to Walnut Ridge _____

2. Oakwood to Willowbrook _____

3. Cypress to Olive _____

4. Magnolia to Mulberry _____

Write the name of the town:

9. _____ is closest to the southeast county border.

10. _____ is closest to the southwest county border.

Write the direction from one town to the other:

5. Redwood Falls is _____ of Aspen.

6. Cypress is ___ _____ of Birch Run.

7. Beechwood is _____ of Magnolia.

8. Forest Hills is _____ of Palm Grove.

Name _____ Date _____

Wheels Away

Eight kids on Schoolhouse Road ride their bikes to school. Use the Wheels Ruler on page 69 to measure the number of feet each rider travels from home to school.

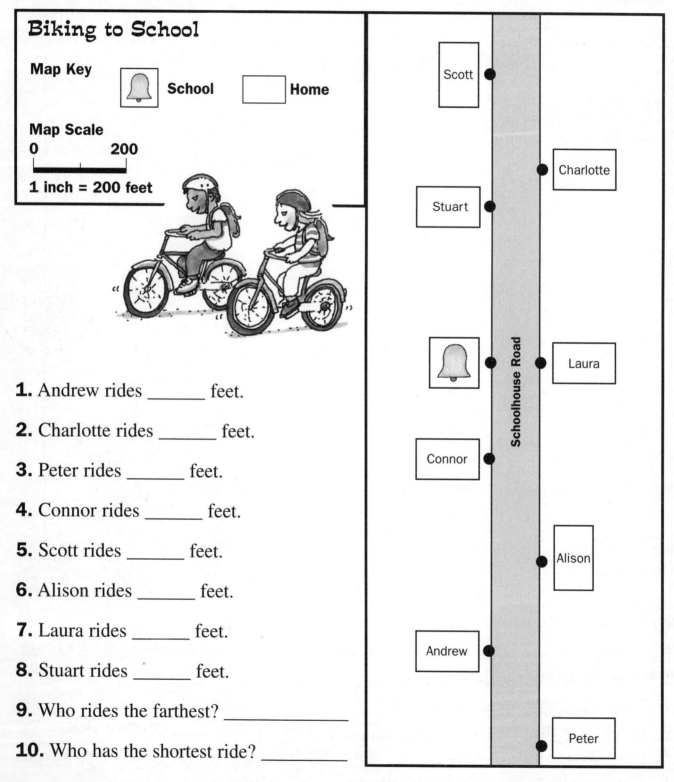

Biking to School

Map Key

🔔 **School**   ☐ **Home**

Map Scale

0   200

1 inch = 200 feet

1. Andrew rides _____ feet.

2. Charlotte rides _____ feet.

3. Peter rides _____ feet.

4. Connor rides _____ feet.

5. Scott rides _____ feet.

6. Alison rides _____ feet.

7. Laura rides _____ feet.

8. Stuart rides _____ feet.

9. Who rides the farthest? _____

10. Who has the shortest ride? _____

Road Rally

The Old Car Road Rally just began. Use the clues below to draw lines on the map and show the rally's route. Use the Road Ruler (page 69) and the map scale to find the distance traveled from town to town. Write each distance next to your lines.

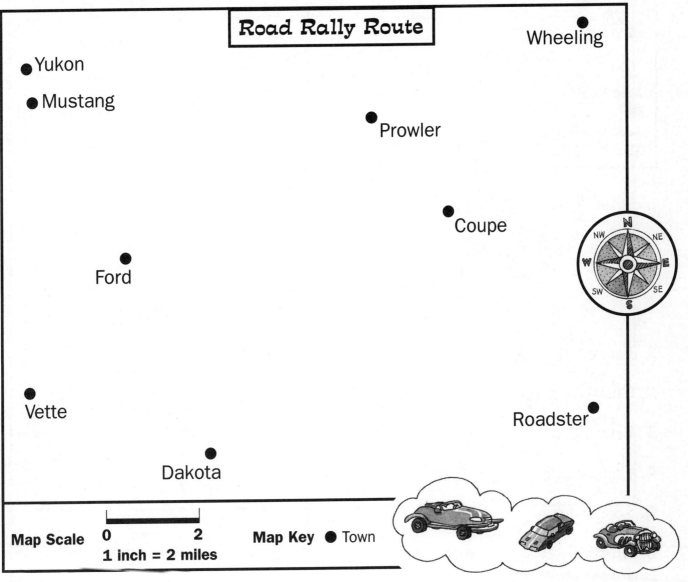

Road Rally Route

Wheeling

Yukon

Mustang

Prowler

Coupe

Ford

Vette

Roadster

Dakota

Map Scale   0   2   Map Key ● Town
              1 inch = 2 miles

Clues

1. The rally started in Yukon. Fifty cars headed _____ miles southeast to Roadster.

2. From Roadster, the cars paraded _____ miles west to _____.

3. From Vette they went 14 miles northeast to _____.

4. From there they turned _____ and drove _____ miles to Dakota.

5. From Dakota they traveled _____ miles northwest to Mustang under a starry sky.

6. The total distance of the road rally was _____ miles.

On the Right Track

Take a train trip on this transportation map to answer the questions below.

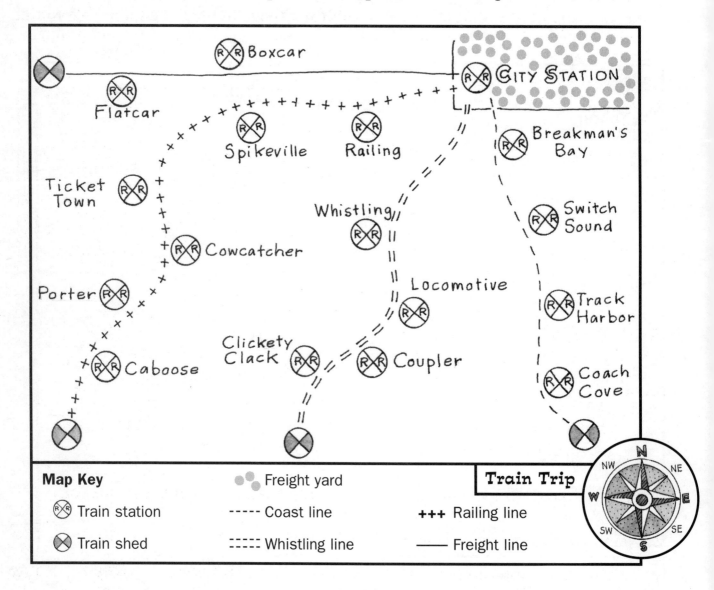

1. What surrounds City Station? _____

2. Which line goes to Clickety-Clack? _____

3. In which direction does the Freight Line run from City Station? _____

4. Which line has the most train stations? _____

5. What is at the end of each line? _____

6. From City Station, what is the third station on the Coast Line? _____

Superb Suburb*

Your job is to create a new community in the suburbs. Make a map to show your "superb suburb" ideas to others. Follow the steps below:

Make a Map

1. Paste or tape the Fit-Together Suburb Map (pages 46–47) side by side.

2. Cut out the blank map key from page 72. Paste it to the bottom of your map.

3. Paste a compass rose from page 73 to the map.

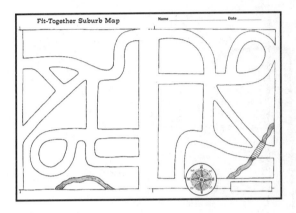

Add Symbols and Details

1. Look at the general, suburb, and abstract symbols on pages 74–76.
Cut and paste symbols of your choice on your map or draw your own.
   • Your community might show neighborhoods with only homes.
   • Some neighborhoods might have a mix of homes and other places.
   A main road might have many places of work along it.

2. Show all your symbols in the map key. Write what each symbol stands for.

3. Name your roads. Some may use these words:

   Street   Lane   Way   Highway   Avenue   Boulevard   Road   Route

4. Write a name for your superb suburb in the title box.

***Use with pages 46–47 and 72–76.**

Fit-Together Suburb Map

MAP SKILLS MADE FUN · NEIGHBORHOODS AND COMMUNITIES *Use with pages 45, 47, 68, and 72–76.

Name _____ **Date** _____

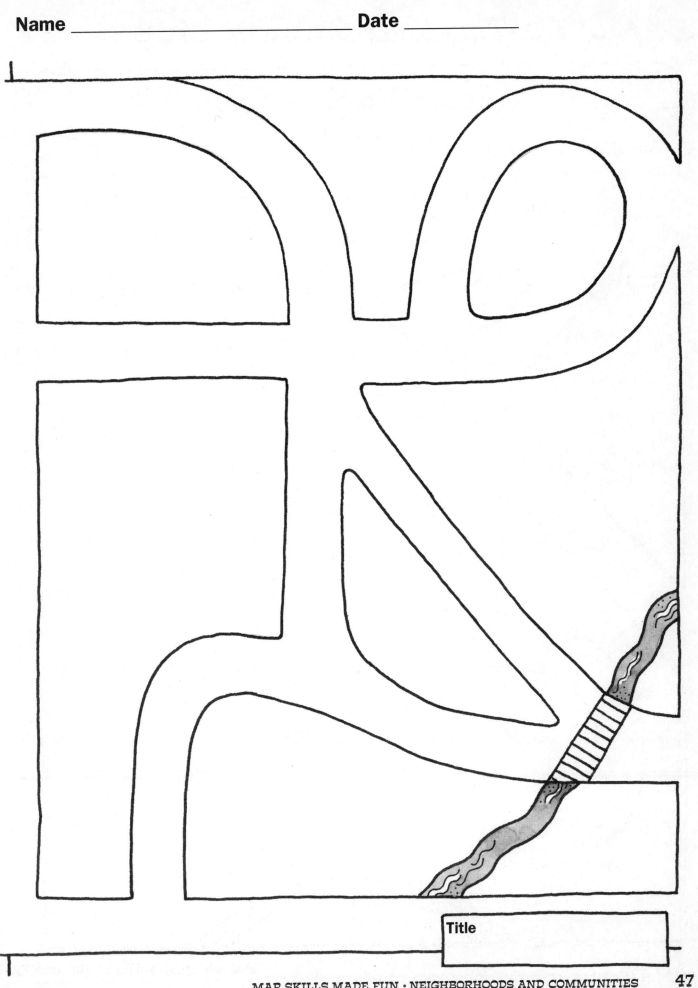

Title

From Eagles' Eyes

As eagles soar high above the rural countryside, they might see places like these. Write what you see from eagles' eyes next to each picture. Then, cut out the mini pages and staple them together to make a mini map book of rural places.

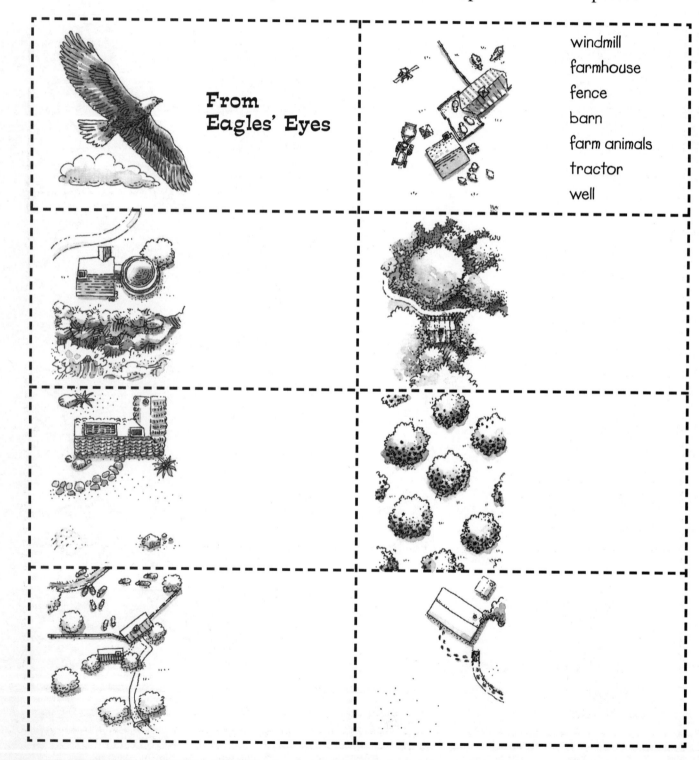

From
Eagles' Eyes

windmill
farmhouse
fence
barn
farm animals
tractor
well

From Eagles' Eyes

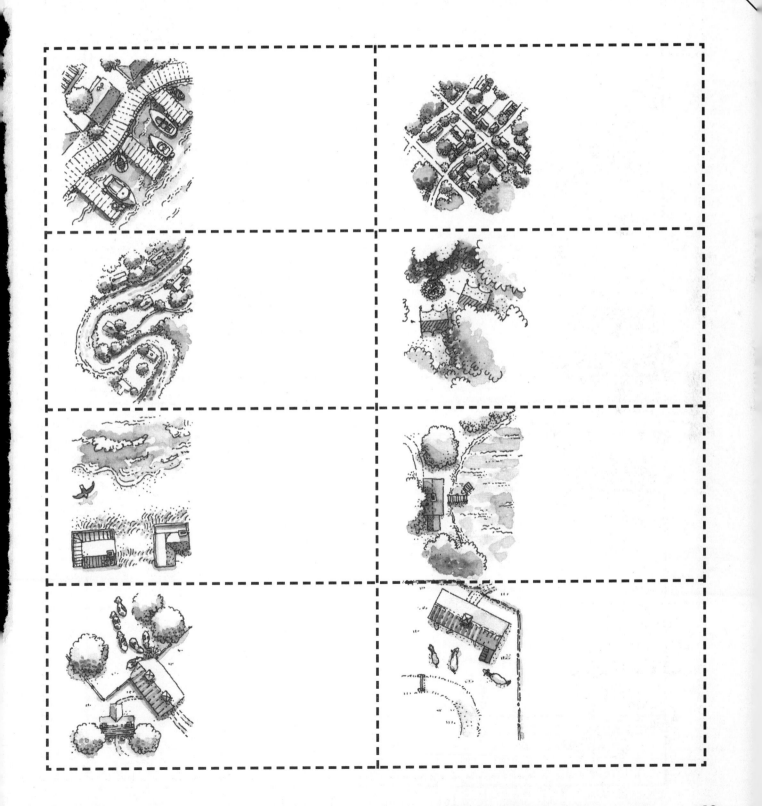

Name _____ **Date** _____

Country Creation

Make a map of this country picture using your own symbols. Draw your symbols in the key and write what each one stands for. Then write a name for your map in the title box.

Title

Map Key

On Main Street

Name _____ **Date** _____

Welcome to Mill Grove! Like many other rural towns, Mill Grove has a main street running through the town's center. Use the map and key below to tell where places are in Mill Grove.

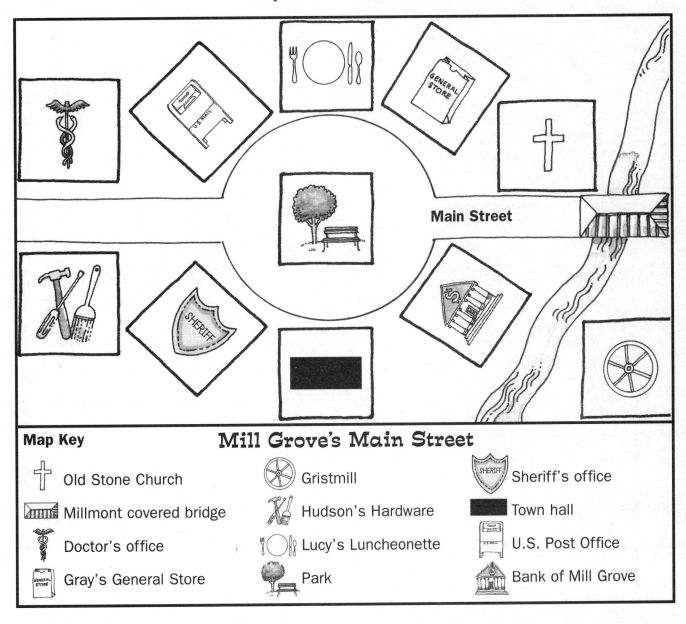

Map Key — **Mill Grove's Main Street**

✝ Old Stone Church   ⊛ Gristmill   🛡 Sheriff's office

▱ Millmont covered bridge   ⚒ Hudson's Hardware   ■ Town hall

⚕ Doctor's office   🍽 Lucy's Luncheonette   ✉ U.S. Post Office

📄 Gray's General Store   🌳 Park   🏛 Bank of Mill Grove

1. The town hall is between the sheriff's office and the _____.

2. A _____ is to the left of the U.S. Post Office.

3. Old Stone Church is to the right of _____.

4. A _____ is in the middle of Main Street.

5. _____ crosses over Mill River.

Saddle Up

This floor plan shows the inside of a barn on Saddler's Farm.
Use the floor plan to answer the questions below.

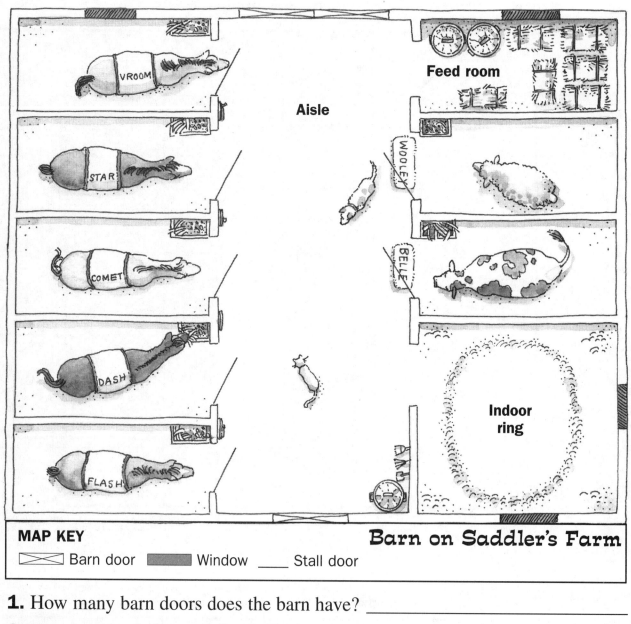

MAP KEY

⊠ Barn door ▨ Window ___ Stall door

Barn on Saddler's Farm

1. How many barn doors does the barn have? _____

2. How many windows are in the room with the indoor ring? _____

3. How many stalls are for horses? _____

4. What is across from Vroom's stall? _____

5. Whose stall is next to Wooley's? _____

6. Where is the barn cat? _____

Down on the Farm

Sickle's Farm is ready for its grand opening. But the farm's map isn't finished! Help complete the map by adding the coordinates of each place to the map index.

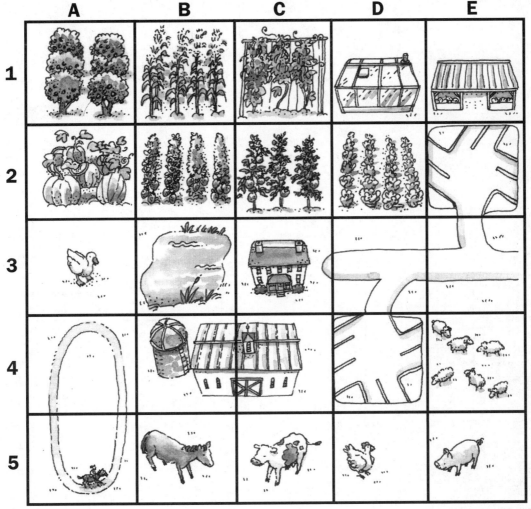

Sickle's Farm

MAP INDEX

Pick Your Own

Apples __1-A__

Corn _____

Lettuce _____

Peas _____

Pumpkins _____

Strawberries _____

Tomatoes _____

Farm Animals

Chickens _____

Cows _____

Ducks _____

Horses _____

Pigs _____

Sheep _____

Other

Farm stand _____

Greenhouse _____

Parking _____

Riding lessons _____

Name _____ **Date** _____

Dino Dig*

Scientists have uncovered dinosaur bones from long ago! Cut out the dinosaur parts and paste them on the Cool Coordinates grid (page 17) to make your own map of the dig site. Then write the coordinates on the map index below and add it to your map.

Map Index

Egg _____

Foot bone _____

Footprint _____

Jaw bone _____

Large tooth _____

Leg bone _____

Rib bone _____

Skull _____

Small tooth _____

Tailbone _____

*Use with page 17.

White Water

Follow the paths of these white-water rafts to answer the questions below.

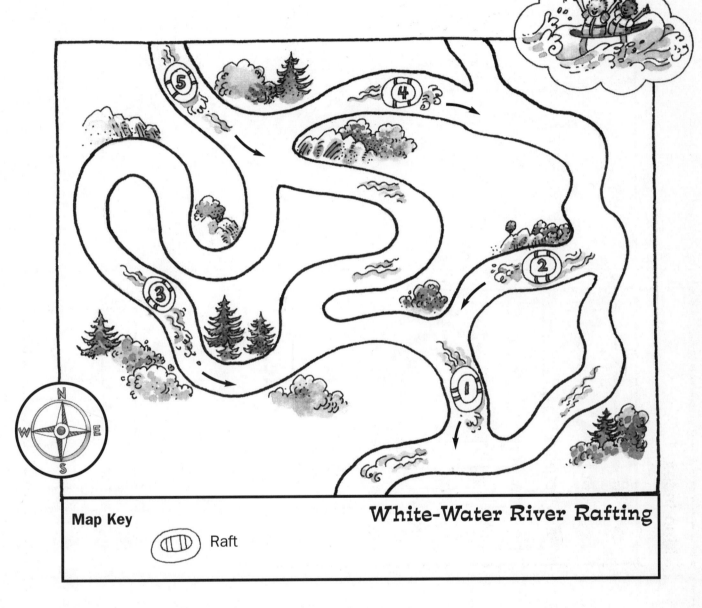

Map Key   **White-Water River Rafting**

⬭ Raft

1. From which direction is Raft 5 riding? _____
2. In which direction is Raft 1 traveling? _____
3. In which direction is Raft 4 traveling? _____
4. In which direction is Raft 2 traveling? _____
5. In which direction will Raft 3 ride next? _____

Tracking Trails

Test your tracking skills. Follow the different trails on this map.
Then use the compass rose and the map to fill in the blanks.

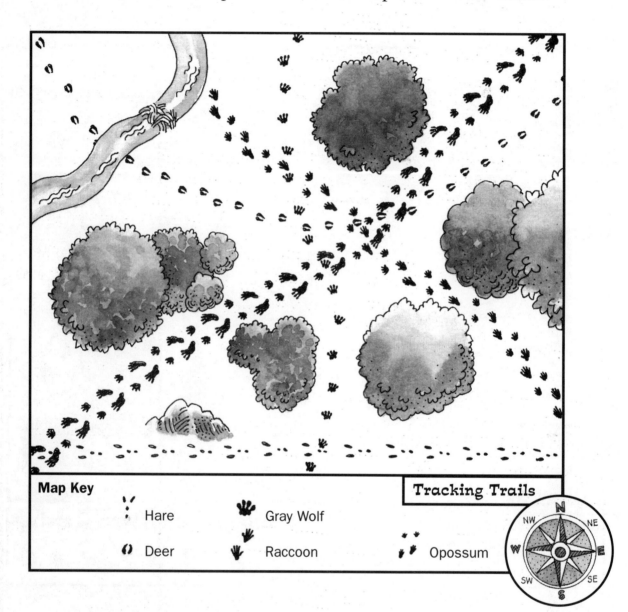

Map Key

Hare   Gray Wolf

Deer   Raccoon   Opossum

Tracking Trails

1. The hare started in the east and is heading _____.

2. The raccoon started in the southeast and is heading _____.

3. The gray wolf started in the south and is heading _____.

4. The opossum started in the northeast and is heading _____.

5. The deer started in the northwest and is heading _____.

Autumn Adventure

In the fall, there are many exciting things to do and buy in rural areas.
Use the map to go on an autumn adventure. Then answer the questions below.

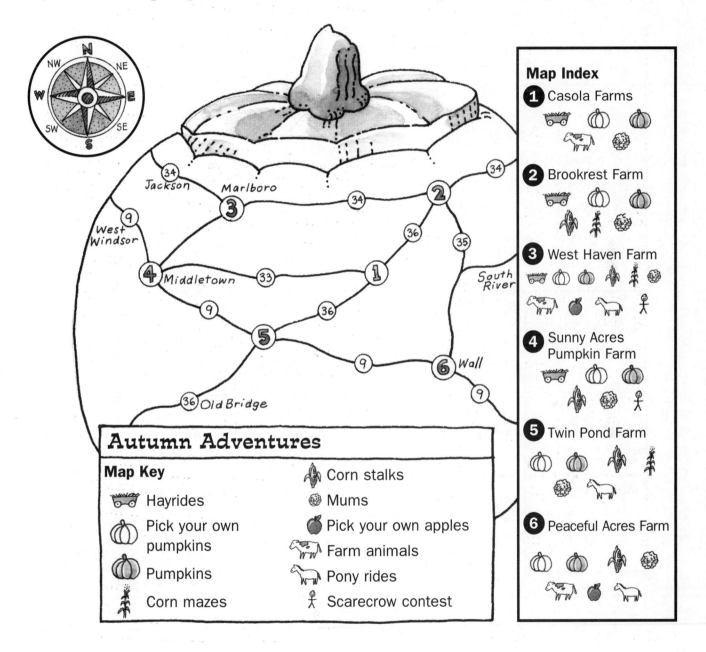

1. Which farm is northeast of Casola Farms? _____

2. Which farm has the most activities and products? _____

3. Which farm on Route 36 has pony rides? _____

4. Which farm on Route 9 has hayrides? _____

5. Do both farms on Route 34 have corn mazes? _____

Directions in Directions*

Use your compass skills and the directions below to color the grid on page 59. Your finished picture will show the answer to this joke:

What naked animal lives near many rural communities? _____

NW corner

- Color the corner box in the NW blue.
- Color 2 1/2 boxes E of this corner blue.
- Color 2 1/2 boxes S of this corner blue.
- Color the box SE of this corner blue.
- Color 1/2 of the box E of the last box blue.

NE corner

- Color the corner box in the NE blue.
- Color 1/2 of the box W of this corner blue.
- Color 1/2 of the box S of this corner blue.

- Color ⬭ black.
- Color one box W, SW, and S of ⬭ brown.
- Color one box to N, W, and SW of ⬭ brown.
- Draw ⬭ to the NW of ⬭ .
- Draw ⬭ to the NE of ⬭ .
- Draw ⬭ in the box E of ⬭.

SW corner

- Color the corner box in the SW brown.
- Color 3 3/4 boxes E of this corner brown.
- Color 2 1/2 boxes N of this corner brown.
- Color the box NE of this corner brown.

SE corner

- Color the corner box in the SE green.
- Color the box N of this corner green.
- Color the box NW of this corner green.
- Color 1/4 of the box W of this corner green.
- Color the third and fourth boxes N of this corner gray.
- Color the box W of each of these last boxes gray.

Directions in Directions

Follow the directions on page 58 to color the grid below.

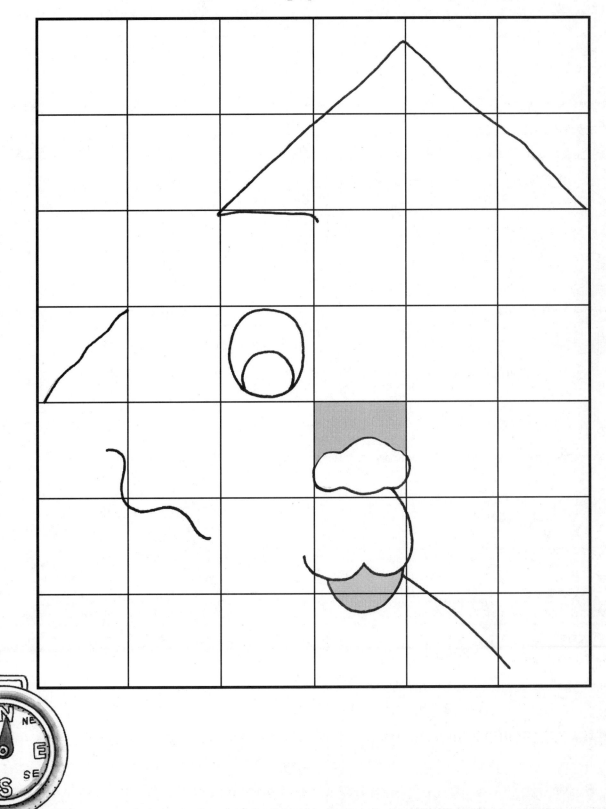

Busting Big Air

Use the Snowball Ruler on page 70 to measure the runs between the snowboarders. Write the number next to each run. Use your numbers to complete the exercises.

Snowboard Runs

1. _____ snowballs between E and F

2. _____ snowballs between G and H

3. _____ snowballs between A and B

4. _____ snowballs between C and D

5. Which snowboarders on the same run are farthest apart? _____

6. Which snowboarders on the same run are closest? _____

Three Peaks

The roads connecting the towns in Peaks County form a land and water picture.
The number of miles between towns is shown next to the roads.

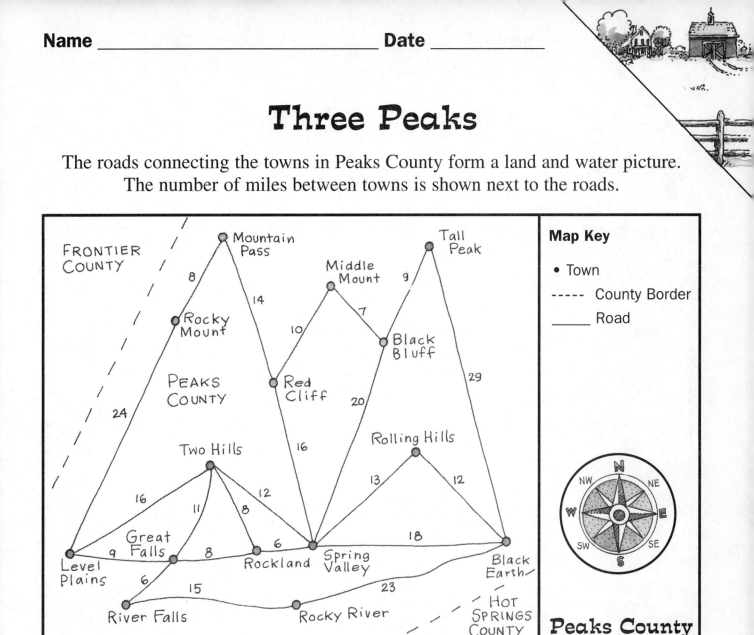

Write the number of miles between these towns:

1. River Falls to Rockland _____

2. Red Cliff to Black Bluff _____

3. Middle Mount to Tall Peak _____

4. Level Plains to River Falls _____

Write the direction from one town to the other:

5. Black Earth is _____ of Level Plains.

6. Rockland is _____ of Two Hills.

7. Rocky River is _____ of Rolling Hills.

8. Rocky Mount is _____ of Great Falls.

Write the name of the town:

9. _____ is nearest the southeast county border.

10. _____ is farthest north in Peaks County.

Desert Sculptures

Use the Cactus Ruler on page 70 to find the distances between
the desert sculptures on this map.

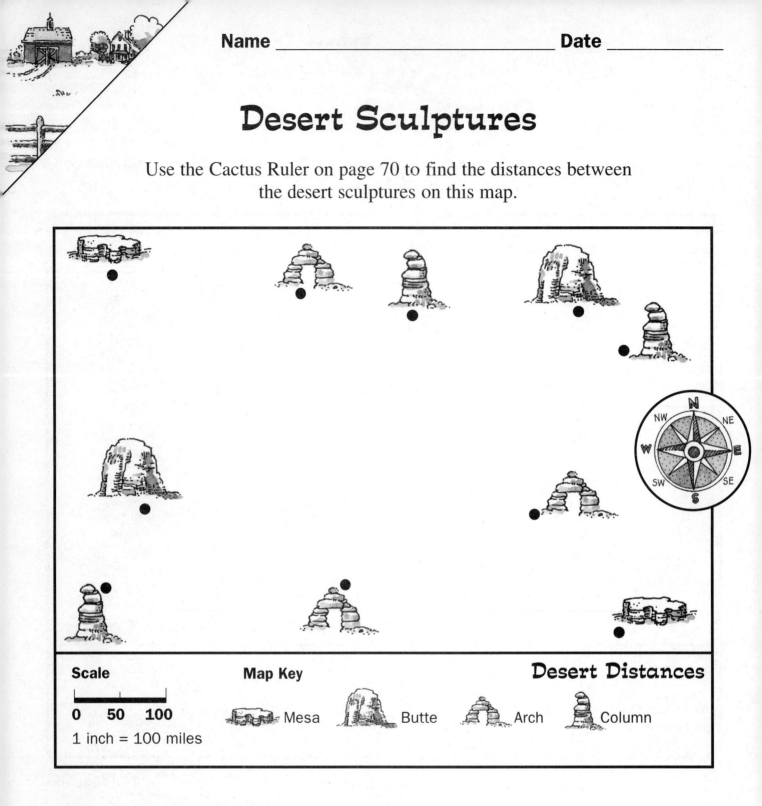

Scale

0   50   100

1 inch = 100 miles

Map Key

Mesa   Butte   Arch   Column

Desert Distances

1. How many miles are between the mesas? _____

2. How many miles are between the buttes? _____

3. How many miles are between the column in the NE and
the column in the SW? _____

4. How far apart are the two closest sculptures? _____

5. Which arch is farther away from the arch in the east? _____

Name _____ **Date** _____

Camp Winaped

Take a walk around Camp Winaped from cabin A to the canoes. Use the
Paddle Ruler on page 70 to find the walking distance from one place to another.

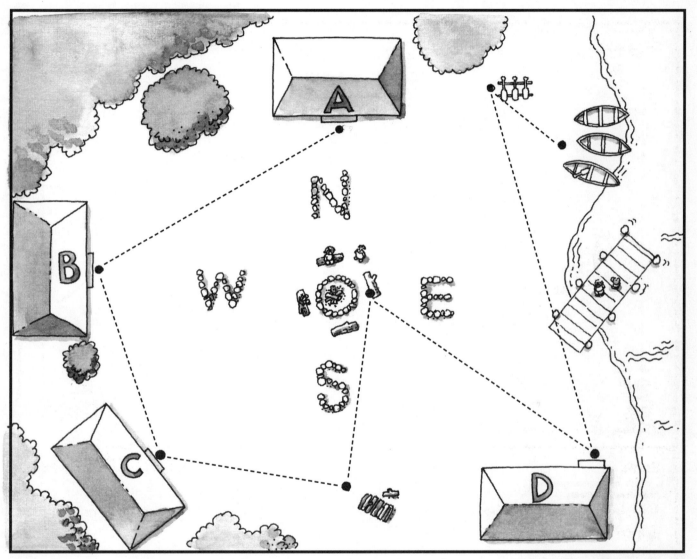

1. _____ feet from cabin A to cabin B
2. _____ feet from cabin B to cabin C
3. _____ feet from cabin C to the log pile
4. _____ feet from the log pile to the campfire
5. _____ feet from the campfire to cabin D
6. _____ feet from cabin D to the paddle rack
7. _____ feet from the paddle rack to the canoes
8. What was the total distance of your walk? _____

Camp Winaped

Scale

0   10

1 inch = 10 feet

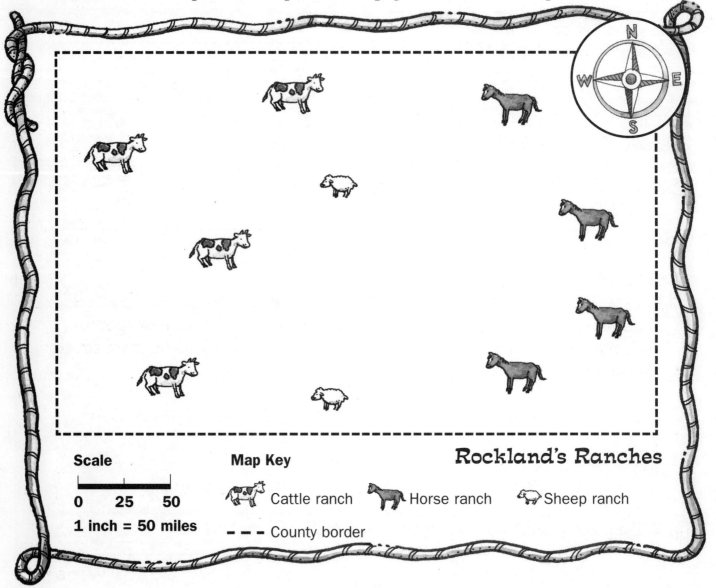

Rockland's Ranches

Ranches are large farms that raise horses, cattle, or sheep. Rockland County has many ranches. Use the map and the Rope Ruler on page 70 to answer the questions below.

Scale

0   25   50

1 inch = 50 miles

Map Key

Cattle ranch   Horse ranch   Sheep ranch

- - - County border

Rockland's Ranches

1. How many horse ranches are in Rockland County? _____

2. What kind of ranches are in the western part of the county? _____

3. What is the distance between the two sheep ranches? _____

4. What is the distance between the north and south county borders? _____

5. What is the distance between the east and west borders? _____

Country Community*

Create a new rural community. Start by making a map to show your ideas to others. Follow the steps below.

Make a Map

1. Paste or tape the Fit-Together Rural Map (pages 66–67) side by side.

2. Cut out the blank map key from page 72. Paste it to the bottom of your map.

3. Paste a compass rose from page 73 to the map.

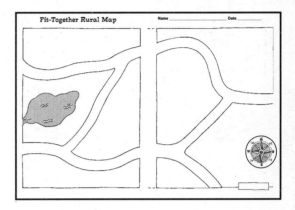

Add Symbols and Details

1. Look at the map symbols on pages 74–76. Cut out and paste symbols of your choice on your map. Draw your own symbols, too. Choose the best spot for each symbol. You might want to show many places of work along main streets. You might place ranches, farms, or homes far apart.

2. Show all your symbols in the map key. Write what each symbol stands for.

3. Name your roads. Some may use these words:

Street   Lane   Way   Highway   Route

4. Write a good name for your country community in the title box.

*Use with pages 66–67 and 72–76.

Fit-Together Rural Map

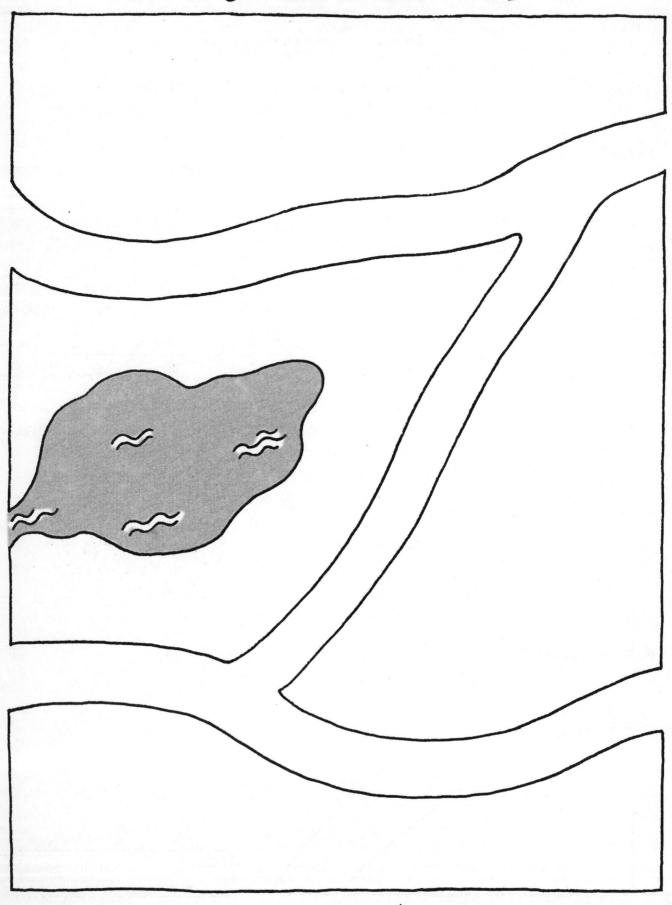

*Use with pages 65, 67–68, and 72–76.

Name _____ Date _____

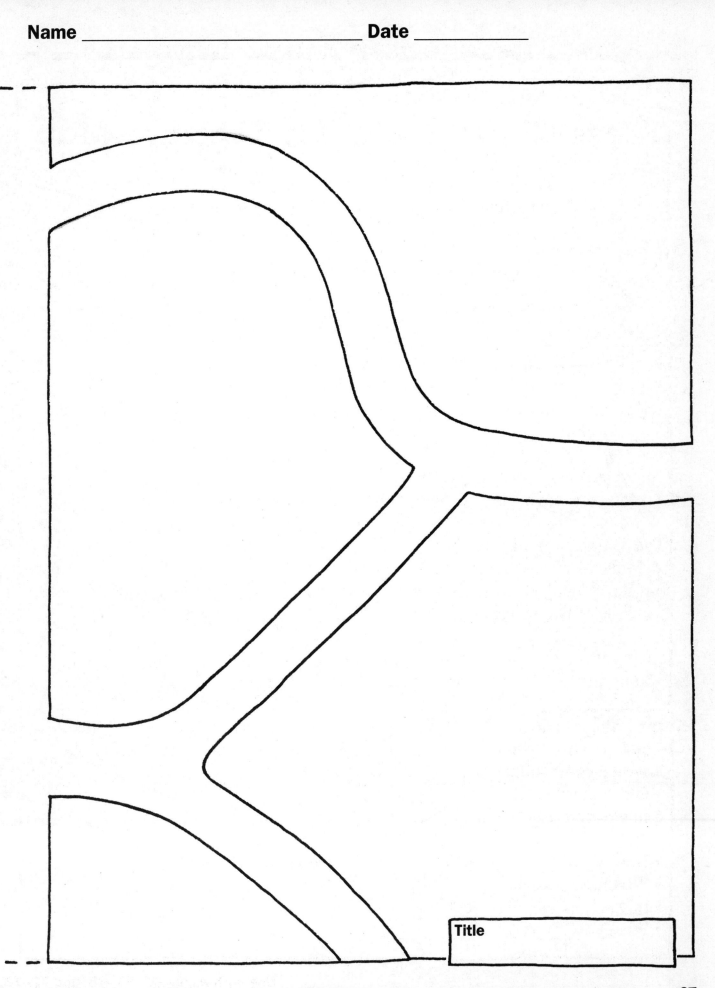

Title

Three Communities Fit-Together Map

You can make one big communities map using the City, Suburb,
and Rural Fit-Together Maps you've already made.

Make Your Map
❏ Paste your suburb map to the right side of your city map.
❏ Paste your rural map to the right side of your suburb map.

Check Your Map
❏ **Name all your roads.**
- New roads were formed when you pasted your maps together.
- Try to use road names that tell about your communities. A road near an apple orchard might be called "Apple Tree Lane."

❏ **Make sure your map keys show all your map symbols.**
- Add symbols you missed. Write what each one stands for.

❏ **Did you use the same symbol on more than one map?**
- If you did, that symbol should stand for the same kind of place or thing on each map.
- If the symbol stands for different places or things, change the look of the symbol on one or two maps. You can also paste over the symbol with a new one.

❏ **Make all new changes on your maps and keys.**
- Your map symbols and key symbols should match.

Write About Your Map
❏ **Your questions should be about places and things in each community.**
- Which community has a _____?
- On what road is a _____?
- In what places can you _____?
- What is next to the _____?
- How many _____ are in the city?
- Which road meets _____?
- In what direction is _____ from _____?
- Where is a _____?

Cut-Out Rulers

Step Ruler (for page 23)

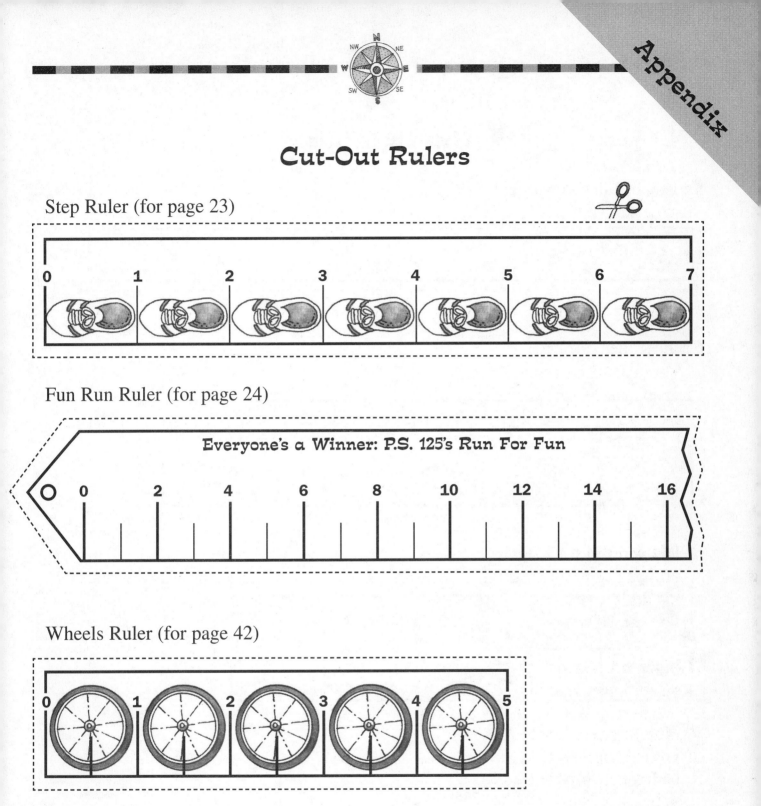

Fun Run Ruler (for page 24)

Everyone's a Winner: P.S. 125's Run For Fun

Wheels Ruler (for page 42)

Road Ruler (for page 43)

Cut-Out Rulers

Snowball Ruler (for page 60)

Cactus Ruler (for page 62)

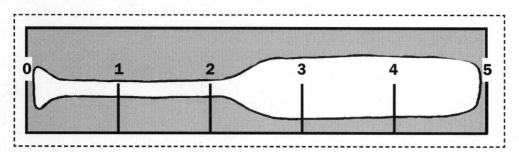

Paddle Ruler (for page 63)

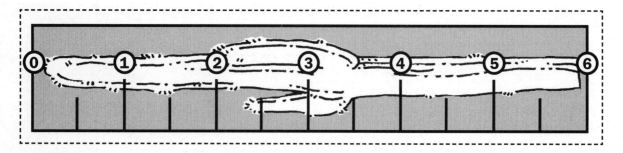

Rope Ruler (for page 64)

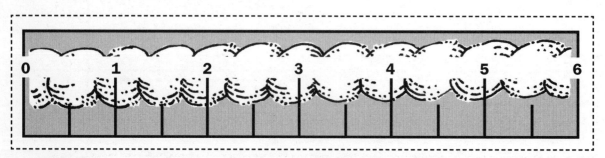

Blank Map Index

Use this map index cutout on any of your community maps.

Map Index

_____   _____

_____   _____

_____   _____

_____   _____

_____   _____

_____   _____

_____   _____

_____   _____

_____   _____

_____   _____

_____   _____

_____   _____

_____   _____

Paste this flap under the side of your map.

Blank Map Key

Use this map key cutout on any of your community maps.

Paste this flap under the bottom of your map.

Map Key

Compass Roses

Use these compass cutouts on any of your community maps.

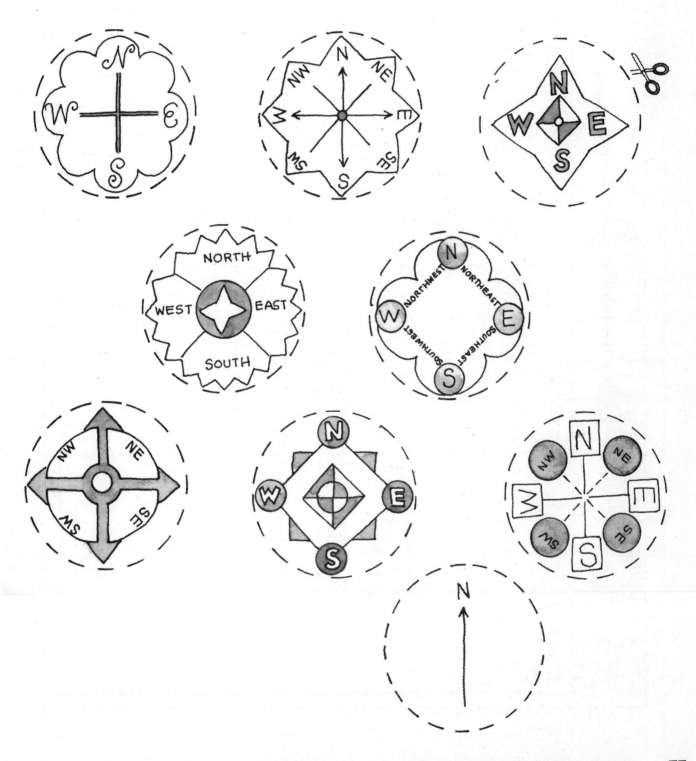

Map Symbols

General Symbols (for city, suburb, and country)

City Symbols

City and Suburb Symbols

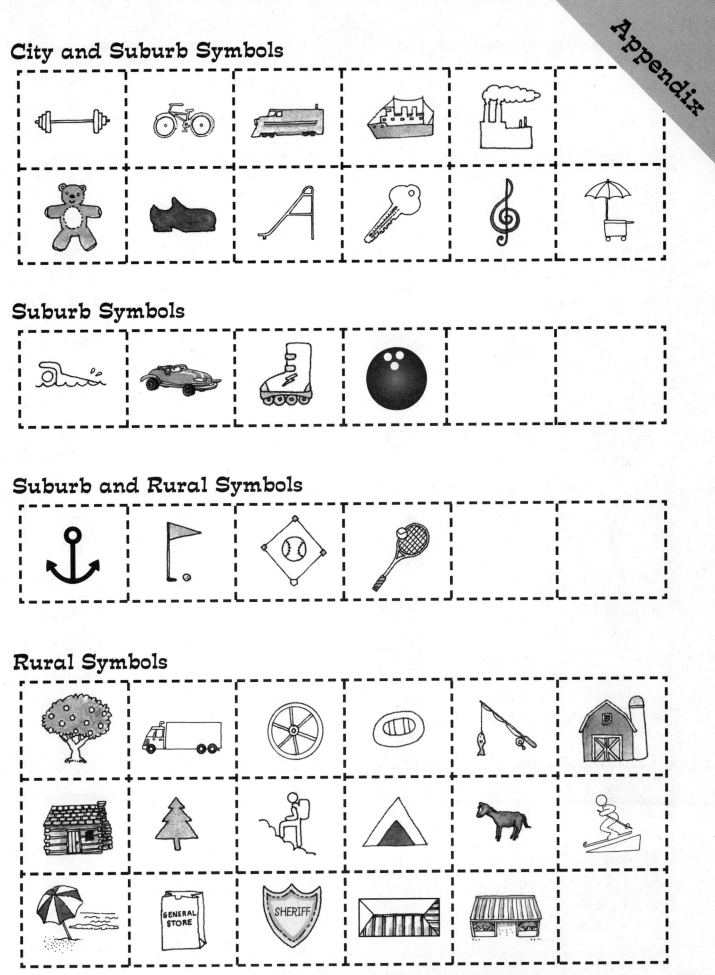

Suburb Symbols

Suburb and Rural Symbols

Rural Symbols

Abstract Symbol Cutouts

These cutouts are abstract symbols. You can use them to stand for different places and things on your community maps.

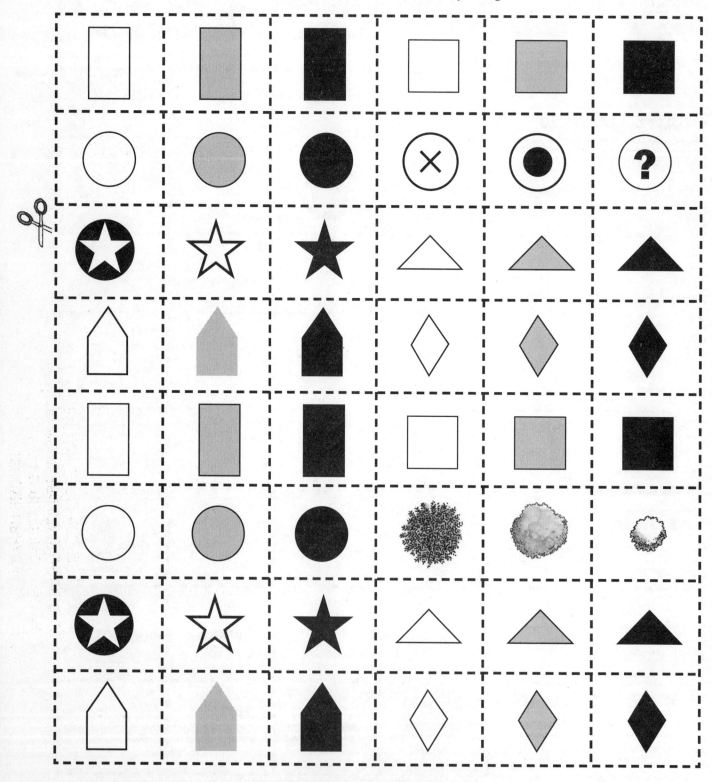

ANSWERS

PART ONE: IN THE CITY

Pigeon's Perch (page 9)

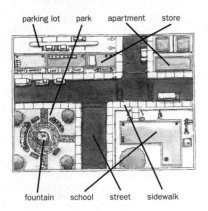

parking lot   park   apartment   store

fountain   school   street   sidewalk

City Sign Language
(page 10)
1. D
2. E
3. F
4. C
5. A
6. B
Children's symbols will vary.

Picture This (page 11)

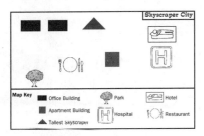

Which Hotel? (page 12)
1. Hotel 206
2. 206 Sleepy Avenue

Missing Exhibits (page 13)
1. totem pole in Native Americans
2. painting in American Presidents
3. hat in American Revolution
4. covered wagon in Pioneers
5. flag in American Flags
6. coin in United States Coins

Zany Zoo (page 14)
Children's symbols should appear as follows:
1-A Zebras
1-B Lions
3-A Gorillas
3-D Reptiles
4-D Polar bears
5-C Penguins
5-D Seals

Eight Steps to City Park
(page 15) Placement of benches, statues, and water fountains may vary.

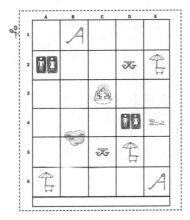

Catch That Bus! (page 18)
1. 1, west
2. 1, north
3. 2, east
4. 2, west

5. 2, south
6. 1, east

Blocks and Lots (page 20)

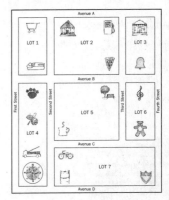

City Sightseer (page 21)
1. 8
2. 10
3. 12
4. 12
5. 20

City to City (page 22)
1. 16
2. 35
3. 13
4. 19
5. south
6. north
7. northeast
8. northwest
9. Red Rock
10. Purpleton

A Step Away (page 23)
1. 300
2. 500
3. 200
4. 600
5. 400
6. 100

ANSWERS

Fun Run (page 24)
300; Avenue A; Cross Street; 700; Avenue B; 1,000; 1,500; Park Place

City Block (page 25)
Maps will vary.

City Planner (page 27)
Maps will vary.

PART TWO: SURROUNDING SUBURBS

Spying Sparrow (page 31)
1 pool
3 dogs
1 cat
1 dog house
1 slide
2 cars
1 umbrella
3 flower gardens
3 trees
1 picnic table
1 swing set
2 chimneys

Picture Perfect (page 32)

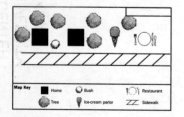

Pirate's Cove Playground (page 33)
1. tube tower
2. seesaw
3. pirate's ship
4. tire swings
5. super slide

Kids' Camp Out (page 34)

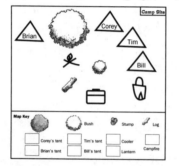

Smart Shopper (page 35)
1. The Candy Jar
2. 9, Toy Masters
3. 4, Hot-Shot Photography
4. 2, Sid's Shoes
5. 1, Sport Spot
6. three

Twin Lakes (page 36)
1. 2-D
2. town
3. Watertown
4. Twin Lakes River
5. Lake Drive
6. 3-C and 3-D
7. 2-B, 2-E, 3-E
8. 2-D, 3-E

Wild Water Park (page 37)
Maps and indexes will vary.

Firefighters' Fair (page 38)
1. north
2. west
3. east
4. east
5. south
6. west

Town Center (page 39)
1. northeast
2. west
3. east
4. north
5. southwest
6. northwest

Perfect Pathways (page 40)
1. 22
2. 23
3. 31
4. 24
5. 25
6. 29
7. 28
8. 29
9. 27
10. path 1
11. path 1
12. path 3

Town to Town (page 41)
1. 8
2. 11
3. 16
4. 17
5. southeast
6. northwest
7. south
8. northeast
9. Evergreen
10. Willowbrook

ANSWERS

Wheels Away (page 42)
1. 600
2. 400
3. 800
4. 200
5. 600
6. 400
7. 100
8. 300
9. Peter
10. Laura

Road Rally (page 43)
star labeled: 14 miles,
12 miles, 14 miles, 12 miles,
8 miles
1. 14
2. 12, Vette
3. Wheeling
4. southwest, 12
5. 8
6. 60

On the Right Track
(page 44)
1. Freight yard
2. Whistling line
3. West
4. Railing Line
5. Train shed
6. Track Harbor

Superb Suburb (page 45)
Maps will vary.

PART THREE: IN THE COUNTRY

From Eagles' Eyes (page 48)
Answers will vary.

Country Creation (page 50)
Children's maps and symbols
will vary.

On Main Street (page 51)
1. Bank of Mill Grove
2. doctor's office
3. Gray's General Store
4. park
5. Millmont Covered Bridge

Saddle Up (page 52)
1. 3
2. 2
3. 5
4. Feed room
5. Belle's
6. Aisle

Down on the Farm (page 53)
Corn 1-B
Lettuce 2-D
Peas 1-C
Pumpkins 2-A
Strawberries 2-B
Tomatoes 2-C
Chickens 5-D
Cows 5-C
Ducks 3-A
Horses 5-B
Pigs 5-E
Sheep 4-E
Farm stand 1-E
Greenhouse 1-D

Parking 2-E, 4-D
Riding lessons 4-A, 5-A

Dino Dig (page 54)
Dig-site maps and indexes
will vary.

White Water (page 55)
1. north
2. south
3. east
4. west
5. east

Tracking Trails (page 56)
1. west
2. east
3. northwest
4. north
5. southwest
6. northeast

Autumn Adventure
(page 57)
1. 2, Brookrest Farm
2. 3, West Haven Farm
3. 5, Twin Pond Farm
4. 4, Sunny Acres Pumpkin
   Farm
5. Yes

ANSWERS

Directions in Directions
(page 59)
A bear

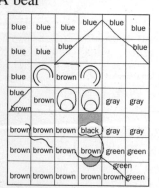

Busting Big Air (page 60)
runs left to right: 6, 5, 7, 8
1. 7
2. 8
3. 6
4. 5
5. G and H
6. C and D

Three Peaks (page 61)
1. 14
2. 17
3. 16
4. 15
5. east
6. southeast
7. southwest
8. north
9. Black Earth
10. Mountain Pass

Desert Sculptures (page 62)
1. 650 miles
2. 500 miles
3. 600 miles
4. 50 miles
5. the north arch

Camp Winaped (page 63)
1. 30
2. 20
3. 20
4. 20
5. 30
6. 40
7. 10
8. 170 feet

Rockland's Ranches
(page 64)
1. 4
2. cattle ranches
3. 100 miles
4. 200 miles
5. 325 miles

Country Community
(page 65)
Maps will vary.

Three Communities
Fit-Together Map (page 68)
Maps will vary.